Life Lived in Reverse

A Memoir

Lucille M. Griswold

Hamilton Books
A member of
The Rowman & Littlefield Publishing Group
Lanham • Boulder • New York • Toronto • Plymouth, UK

Copyright © 2009 by
Hamilton Books
4501 Forbes Boulevard
Suite 200
Lanham, Maryland 20706
Hamilton Books Acquisitions Department (301) 459-3366

Estover Road
Plymouth PL6 7PY
United Kingdom

All rights reserved
Printed in the United States of America
British Library Cataloging in Publication Information Available

Library of Congress Control Number: 2009922920
ISBN: 978-0-7618-4493-8 (paperback : alk. paper)
eISBN: 978-0-7618-4494-5

Front cover photos: Top right, Lu sitting on window sill on Honeymoon in Bermuda, 1953. Left, Lu a college student standing behind a stack of books, 2006. Bottom right, Lu at graduation in front of College Hall, July 18, 2007.

Back cover photo: Lucille sitting on deck rail in Maryland, 2008.

∞ ™ The paper used in this publication meets the minimum requirements of American National Standard for Information Sciences—Permanence of Paper for Printed Library Materials, ANSI/NISO Z39.48-1992.

This book is dedicated to all the wonderful women of my generation who have a story to tell but may be reluctant to tell it. Let this book be the inspiration you need to document your own life story for prosperity and as a legacy for your loved ones.

Contents

Preface		vii
Acknowledgments		xiii
Introduction		1
1	Trauma Years	3
2	Becoming a Jersey Girl	6
3	Outside Influences	9
4	Learning to Make Tough Choices	11
5	Multiple War Years	14
6	Sources of Strength	18
7	Italian Americanness	21
8	My Transient Life	27
9	Being a Woman	31
10	Living the Good Life	51
11	Times to Laugh	54
12	Griswold Vacations	56
13	Learning to Endure	61
14	Simple Times	65

15	Establishing a Lifestyle	69
16	Feeling Italian	75
17	Proud to be an Italian American	81
18	Becoming an Author	84
19	Some Fascinating Women	90
Epilogue		93
Bibliography		95

Preface

"Inside every older lady is a younger lady — wondering what the heck happened."

(Cora Harvey Armstrong)

I am going to start right out by saying I am 73 years old. I have been keeping this something of a secret the last two years. As an online student at Vermont College I kept my age a secret because, for one reason, I didn't want to discourage any younger students who were hoping for a buddy with whom to communicate to find out that they got this little old lady instead. Many of the older students in the Virtual Vermont classroom this year (2007) called themselves "late bloomers," but I knew in my case this was not really true. I was a budding bloomer, both mentally and physically, since about the age of thirteen years old, and my intention always was to get a degree, but life got side-tracked along the way. Instead of having an empty nest syndrome I was the one to leave my last child. I had books published and then went to college to study writing. I became a leader of women and gave speeches without ever having been trained in public speaking. I lived a full exciting life and then reverted back to complete my education. My life was a series of living life in reverse. I will be explaining my journey about this adventure in the memoir to follow, but first I would like to express a few thoughts about my online education and how I got to this point.

Believe it or not, I still have about four friends with whom I went to kindergarten, and even though we live all over the United States we manage to keep in contact with one another. After our fiftieth high school reunion, this small group decided to have a mini reunion, and one of the girls from Texas came to stay with me in Maryland. We then traveled to New Jersey to meet the others. During our conversation in the car, I learned my friend had completed her education at a college in Vermont where she only had to go to class a couple of weeks out of the year, and then do the rest of her study at home and mail her packets (by snail mail). Math and money were the two things keeping me from returning to school, but the more we talked, and the more she explained this wonderful innovative program, the more I became interested. Having made more inquiry with the Vermont College officials I heard I could get an education all online and this idea seemed marvelous. After all, I could send e-mail, right? Online education should be a snap. To say I was naïve would be extremely understated.

I applied and got accepted, and was then told to review the orientation site to see if my computer was equipped to handle the online routine. I looked at all this "stuff" about zip files, java web, and this file and that file and my heart sank. So, I asked my trusty son-on-law if I had all the criteria they said I needed. He assured me that he had long ago set my computer so that everything was up to date, and I was good to go. I enrolled, and the adventure began.

I began to notice a rather pleasant pattern about this method of study that was so reassuring. No one ever got upset with me. They were not so pleasant to me because of my age either since most did not know how old I was. In fact, I would privately get embarrassed when some of my professors would say to me, "Well, we are about the same age," because of something I would write when I was often twelve or more years older than them. Then one professor came right out and asked me how old I was and I told her. She explained I should reveal my age as she felt I would be a good influence, or be an inspiration to the younger students, but I was not so sure.

I had completed one full year of college after high school and was not back in a classroom until over thirty-two years later around 70 years old. I took a women's literature course at the local community college. Those students were absolutely fabulous to me. They would choose me if they needed a partner. They complimented me on my shoes or clothes and made my experience a marvelous one. I remember the first day wondering what to wear for an old lady in school when on campus I passed a lady (who I indeed later found out was close to 90 years old) in a tube top and shorts. At that point I figured there was no way I could go wrong with my attire. She was someone who came to campus to dabble in the art studio.

What a morale booster at the end of the class when I met with the professor to get my final grade. He said he thought I was only fifty. I wrote this poem about my experience:

SCHOOL DAYS

She was an aging senior who decided to go back to school
Her grandchildren questioned her as though she were a fool
She actually liked the study, the work filled her with glee
But one of her biggest worries was that during class she'd have to pee
So many things were obstacles to get this education
Especially when she had to miss the class
For her granddaughter's graduation
She and the other students got along just fine
They thought their professor really hot
But Grandma appreciated his quiet demeanor
She liked that about him a lot
A big surprise to boost her ego though
Were words that were so nifty
When the professor said with quiet shock
He thought her only fifty
The best part of the whole experience
That really made her day
Was the fact that the hot professor
Had given her an "A!"

My first residency at Virtual Vermont was filled with a lot of students who had drug and abuse problems, and when they were telling their tales in the discussion areas I began to think I didn't belong there. They had suffered so much and I admired them so, but I was a relatively happy person and I thought they would not like me at all – not to mention my old age even. I began to think of the things in my life that had been difficult for me. If I found out I had enough of these difficulties then I could say I suffered too, because we all do suffer in one way or another. I was never abused though, so I strangely didn't feel deserving. However, I also know that because of my age I don't belong to the "confessional culture" that is so prevalent today. For me, there are certain topics I will consider socially taboo and these I will not include in my memoir or in my classroom discussions.

Those first few weeks I was on the phone a lot with the technical staff. They were always so very kind. Math and Aesthetics were two requirements I needed to complete, so I made sure that I got those subjects taken care of as soon as possible. I did not realize that when I received a packet response that I was not supposed to send it right back. When I was studying Women's Behavior and exploring Women's Choices, my Professor Sue Cobb would make suggestions and I took them to be corrections. I made all the changes and bounced the work right back to her. I am sure I overwhelmed her, but she kindly told me the proper way to do things and I finally began to settle down, at least in my school life. My personal life started off with a big bang that year and our family was in such turmoil I was nearly thrown off course, but I persisted.

The second semester started with a snowstorm just at the point in the residency where I was given my new professor Laura Knott Twine. My electric power went out and I could not get online – this with an online education. When I finally did get online I was going around greeting all the fellows in my class as I did in the residency, and I did this without reading the instructions because I was so flustered about my late start. My poor Professor telephoned me and asked me why I was bouncing all over the place. We got all that straightened out, but where the first semester started out with a personal obstacle in my life the second semester was filled with a husband who had colon cancer, and I was discovered to have squamous cell carcinoma. I ended up the semester with a major operation. Just before the Christmas holidays we had the shocking death of a favorite nephew. I have this strange habit of not liking to talk about my personal problems thinking that others probably have it worse, so for the most part I kept this information quiet (which is something you can do with an online education) as I knew others had enough problems of their own.

The computer was another thing. When I was told to copy and paste, I was scared to death of the little scissors that showed up on my screen. I thought I was going to lose everything. I never had any formal computer training. All I learned was by hit or miss. I took typing in high school, therefore my speed in typing on the computer shocks even my own children, but that was basically all I knew how to do. Then I had to do the headers and footers. I could figure that a header went at the top of the page, and a footer at the bottom, but how to get this to happen was beyond me. I asked questions and managed to get a header in place, then I made a mistake, and I could not delete the error. Not even my computer-savvy relatives could remove it. Many times I just wanted to pick up the computer and throw it out the window. I would get up and leave and go for a walk, clear my head, and ask more questions. By the end of my third semester I was doing Power Point. Now I just have to remember how to do it again. These "senior" brains can be very trying.

Having always been fascinated by my female friends, and some of the choices they made, I decided to study Women's Choices my first semester. That study only titillated my brain to want to know even more about our gender as I studied the total woman through her ethnicity. I further investigated what caused a woman to establish her identity, and the rites of passage from young adult to an adult woman. My studies also discovered the importance of a woman's upbringing and cultural background. I learned to weigh information received, with reservations, to form my own opinion from what was dispensed through my statistical studies. I photographed working women in all types of professions to give me an aesthetic view of their inner beauty. While doing all of this I kept imagining myself in the position of the women about whom I was studying. This naturally led me to want to compare my own choices, my identity, and my cultural Italian American background. I came to the conclusion that there would be no better way to do this then to end my studies by doing a memoir. This was certainly a new and perhaps difficult undertaking, but in the words of Albert Einstein (1875-1955), the famous theoretical physicist, "Anyone who has never made a mistake has never tried anything new." I will examine my mistakes and my achievements and be happy to know that I was not afraid to try.

I am finally a culminator. The end is in sight. I must confess, at the beginning of this culminating semester I began to question why I wanted to write a memoir and to wonder how I was going to manage reading around 27 books in a 20-credit semester. The journey though has been worth every minute, and I certainly did not make it alone.

Bill, my wonderful husband of 53 years, who was also my high school sweetheart, has been my biggest supporter. He returned to work after many years of retirement in order to pay my tuition, and not at the prestigious professional job he once had. My four children and their spouses have been behind me all the way. What can I say about my twelve grandchildren? Naturally, I think they are superb. Two have already graduated from college, and six more are on the way to graduating. In fact, three of my granddaughters are graduating along with me in the year 2007. We have had a ball comparing our educations and professors. All three of them are going on to graduate school. To those students at Vermont College who were always so kind to me and sent me e-mail notes of encouragement – you are the best!! To the wonderfully understanding, intelligent, and compassionate professors, I send my heartfelt thanks, especially to Professor Cathy Stanton whose assistance with my memoir was invaluable. Last, but certainly not least, I give my thanks to Vermont College of Union Institute & University. You are to be commended for your staff, your excellent professors, your genuine interest in your students, and your innovative program. By accepting me into your school, and supporting me all the way with sincerity and compassion, I have become an invigorated woman with an added sparkle to my life. You helped me to achieve the self-validation I have been seeking my whole life by offering me the type of adult education that made learning fun as well as educationally enticing. This education was the main spark that gave me the incentive to want to reverse my life and start over – to live my life in reverse.

Acknowledgments

Sometimes we become who we are just by our association with wonderful people in our lives. I would like to give mention to those special people because without this association I most likely would not have been the person I am today.

I would first like to thank my Publisher, Hamilton Books of the University Press of America, for having the gumption to publish a positive story and not one about dysfunction. I commend you for this, and I also appreciate the guidance provided by Judith Rothman, Patti Belcher, Brian DeRocco and Brooke Bascietto.

To "Mem" Campbell (thanks to you I got my degree), Jeanette Masia, Dot Davino (recently deceased) and Carole Hicks (friends since kindergarten), and Peggy Deitz, my dear friend since grammar school. How wonderful to not only grow up with you, but to still have most of you in my life today.

To my military wife friends–Jan Brady, Barbara Rock, Barbara Molino, Mary Devlin, Betty White and Joanne Martin, many of whom are also in my book club. We are representatives of the Army, Coast Guard and Navy. We have "been there and done that," and we understand each other like no other group of women possibly can.

To Judy, Jan, Carol, Sue, Liz D., Liz F., Rita, Barbara H., Nancy K., Barbara R., Nancy S., Dotty, Betty, Mary and Betsy–my friends from the Chapeau Rouge Mesdames who add to my joie de vivre.

To Fran Marshall, who came into my life as an adult, but our bond is as strong as if I knew you forever, along with Betty Licitra, Annette Markellos, Joanne Behanna, Mae Tarasuk, Fran Digiacomo and Colleen Seyl.

To Jheremy – together we prove that age has no barriers in friendship.

To Vicky Szirbik and Lenella Miller—I will always be grateful for your kind words of encouragement and your support when we were all at Virtual Vermont.

To two fantastic Professors, Cathy Stanton and Laura Knott Twine, whose guidance and patience I will always appreciate.

To my cousins Ruth Ann Mackway, Louis Mazzei and Alfred Ewington—It's fun to share our memories of the house on Broad Street and the people we loved there.

To my husband's cousin LaVerne McCloskey. We married the same year and have the bond of sharing many personal pleasures and heartaches together.

To my Aunt Gloria Mennie—You are my special and adoring link to my father.

Every family event is unique when associating with my husband's siblings, Marlene Anderson, Joan Wolf, and Jim Griswold and their spouses George, Bill and Patricia and the great nieces and nephews. No one laughs as hard as we do when we are together.

To my wonderful sons Gary and Greg, and magnificent daughters Pam and Sandy - I can't think of how special you are to me without getting tears in my eyes. Your spouses are like my own children-Lore, Sarah, Keith and Mike (recently deceased). You all always know the right things to do and say. I will always be thankful for your faith in me and your kind support.

To Cheyne, Bryan, Cathy, Devina, Amanda, Aaron, Ashley, Robert, Teresa, Brandi, Camille and Mikey—I was born on the 12th day of the 12th month, so is it any wonder that I hit the jackpot with 12 beautiful grandchildren. You are my pot of gold at the end of the rainbow.

And especially to my husband Bill—my life was made special because you were there beside me since we were thirteen years old. God gave me a "jewel" when he gave me you.

Introduction

Imagine you have reached the pinnacle of your life. Imagine all the dreams you had of a lovely home and family came true. Imagine living and/or traveling to many different continents and all of the fifty United States of America. Imagine spending your winter in warm climates where your spouse can get in all the golfing he wants because you are both retired. Imagine living in high society and being entertained by queens and high-ranking officials from foreign countries and your own United States. Imagine loving every minute of what you have achieved. Then imagine that this really did happen, and yet you decided to go back and live your life in reverse. This is exactly what happened when I told my husband I wanted to go back to school and finally get my Bachelor's Degree. I guess you could say I would rather live my life in reverse instead of In Memoriam.

My husband and I were having a pleasant conversation one morning. We both loved being retired and doing things we darned well pleased. We agreed that if we were to die the next day we would have no regrets since we had lived a good life. Yet, there had been something nagging at my mind since I had recently heard of a new form of online adult education at Vermont College. I never had "my turn" to complete my education. Women have a way of worrying that they are being selfish when it comes to spending family money on themselves (my studies have proven that), and I was no different. When we were younger, there were no FASFA loans, nor other opportunities to get educational loans. My spouse and I married young. We knew one of us needed an education, so we put all our effort into getting him eight years of education after high school to become a professional prosthodontist. He also had two more years of specialty training at Tripler Army Medical Center Hospital in Hawaii for which we did not have to pay. A prosthodondist does the type of dentistry that makes your mouth beautiful by doing extensive bridgework, veneers and implants. It took us seventeen years to pay off his education and then it was time to start paying for our oldest son's education. We ended up paying for a total of twenty-five years of education for my husband and all our children. Since we decided to marry young, we did not expect our parents to pay for any of this, and they did not. In retrospect, some of those early years without money were some of the best in our lives.

I began to feel the time had come to finally complete my own education. I began taking courses at the local community college and some courses at the University of Maryland, but something about learning at Virtual Vermont in Vermont College was more than appealing. When I first mentioned my worry about getting money for my education, the financial aid people told me that it would be discrimination to refuse me a scholarship or loan because of my age, so I felt rather confident applying for two scholarships being offered for older women. I got a glowing evaluation from my then professor, and prior employers, only to be refused. These were corporations that gave out scholarships in the amount of $10,000 and they could not even see fit to give me even $1,000. You cannot tell me prejudice was not involved. Some of the women board members who made the decision were about the age of some of my children, so I felt a little sad that they could not see beyond the stereotypical college student. It was not as though these loans were going to be given to young students who still had a future ahead of them since they were specifically established for older students. Not even the National Italian-American Foundation saw fit to offer me any money, and I am Italian on both my mother's and father's side. However, once they had my name they kept inviting me to these expensive functions. If I had the money those functions required I would not have been seeking financial aid from them. Often, these organizations rely a lot on volunteer work being documented. We are the type of people, except for having publicly volunteered at my church for years, who do volunteer work that is not highlighted by publicity. If we know a poor family is in need, we stick money in an envelope and ask our priest to give the money to that family. With twelve grandchildren we are constantly giving of our time and money. I prepare meals for families incapable of doing so or have worked at women's shelters and had been an active Red Cross Volunteer for many years. We always helped with Scouting and Little League sports. We do not seek personal recognition, so this is rather hard to document on a form for others to praise. My husband was determined that we would not reach into our retirement funds, so he went out and joined the work force again to pay for my education. Is that a love story or what? Corny though it may sound, this is exactly how it happened. At a family dinner one evening my twenty-one year old grandson said, when he was shocked to hear his Pops had gone back to work driving a school bus, "Gosh Mom-Mom, it is as though you and Pops are starting over." In many ways he was right.

Chapter One

Trauma Years

One day when I was about four years old, for some reason I never found out, my mother and I moved into my grandparents' household. Many families have secrets that fester for years, but in this case I do not really believe it was any big secret why my Mom left our prior home and my father. I believe if I had asked I would have been given a reason. I just never bothered to question what had happened since everyone seemed happy and content in my new home. I saw my father only on rare occasions after that. He used to live in another town and he was respected in his community. His looks resembled the actor Al Pacino. I remember my father played a mandolin and he always looked happy, but I don't remember getting gifts from him. No one ever explained to me what happened, or why, and frankly, since nothing appeared in my little life to be wrong, I was not bothered by this situation. When I look back and hear these people on Oprah saying their lives were ruined without a mother or a father in their lives, I think it odd that I was never affected by this loss. For years when we drove by a beautiful luxurious hotel in Asbury Park, New Jersey, I would hear the family remark that this is where my parents Ruth and Mike got married, but that is about all I ever knew about their lives together. I have a wedding photo that shows a large wedding party and the bridesmaids carrying enormous bouquets of fresh flowers.

Our household consisted of my grandmother, grandfather, great-grandfather, three aunts (my mother's sisters), my mother and me. Don't ask me how, but this combination of people living together worked. My grandparents had their own room, as did my great-grandfather. The three sisters shared another room. My mother and I shared a tiny room, with cot-like beds, that was bright and cheery with white net curtains at the window that overlooked the lawn where we used to play croquet, and I could watch them cutting the grass with a push lawnmower. For eleven years, throughout my childhood in the 1940's,

I was the only grandchild and they doted upon me. Others in the household may have fought amongst each other, but no one fought with me. I felt a lot of love in that house. Growing up in this atmosphere taught me many valuable lessons. The most prevalent message was to have respect for the elderly and to respect each other's privacy. When my first son was born we had five living generations of my family on my mother's side.

Around the age of seven a distant trauma had a deep effect on me. We used to sit around the radio on Sunday afternoons listening to radio shows called *The Green Hornet* and *The Shadow*. One Sunday afternoon on December 7, 1941, we heard President Roosevelt tell of the bombing of Pearl Harbor. When I learned of the implications of the President's announcement, I realized a fear I had never experienced before. We would sit in the eerie dark during air raid drills, always wondering if this were the time the enemy would drop bombs on our homes. Our family became very involved in the war effort. We used to call my mother "Ruthie the Riveter" because of her taking a job at a defense plant. Today, she and others like her are honored at the Rosie the Riveter memorial in California. During World War II, an unprecedented number of American women responded to government encouragement to enter the high-paying world of the heavy war-production industry. Women who had worked at "pink-collar" jobs (secretaries, waitresses, or other clerical jobs), or in lower-paying women's industrial jobs, flocked to war production work as an opportunity to learn new skills and make higher wages. I know my mother always worked outside the home, but I never paid much attention to the type of work she did. I remember her job as a riveter because she worked a night shift and was driven to work by our next-door neighbor. I can assume that the higher pay was a great motivation to take this job. The family was totally interested in her being a maverick and doing something entirely different. The women in war production work were essentially forced to leave their jobs when the war ended and the men came home.

I would go along to help my great-aunt spot foreign planes. We would stand on wooden platforms that were situated near the remote country roads not far from our homes. Fortunately, we never did spot any foreign enemy planes. This was a good way for me to learn about volunteering our time. In fact the whole community would help in the war effort. Mothers with sons in the service would have flags in their windows with stars. If the flags had gold stars on them, it signified that a loved one had been killed in the war. Children brought scrap metal and foil gum wrappers to school to be recycled into material for airplanes and other war items. We were encouraged to save our nickels and dimes to buy war bonds. Victory gardens freed labor, transportation and funding for the war effort. My grandfather portioned a large section of our yard for all sorts of fresh grown vegetables. The entire country was mobilized in World War II. This is so unlike the situation in Iraq today where most of us do nothing unless we have someone fighting there.

We often had drills in the schools where we had to hide under our desks or squat against the walls in the hallways. One evening during an air raid drill in our darkened home, my grandmother fell against the marble fireplace and cut her face. All the women in the house let out a scream, prompting the air raid warden (our next door neighbor) to knock on our door to see if everything was all right. An unfortunate incident also related to the war occurred when I went to visit my aunt who lived in Ohio. We went on a train, and I remember the fascination of seeing the Horseshoe Bend where the train went around tracks on the side of a mountain in the shape of a horseshoe. I looked forward to going with my aunt that I loved a lot, but I remember the sadness I felt leaving my mother and other family members. I believe if I suffered anything from not having a father it was separation anxiety whenever I had to leave someone close, or they left me, and this happened to occur frequently in my later life.

Many foods were in short supply during the war. My mother used to make butter with white margarine and yellow food coloring. Staples like sugar were rationed for the consumer during the war with each household getting a book of stamps or coupons used to purchase these items. My aunt sent me to the store to buy some sugar and I rode a bike. After I made the purchase, I put the book of stamps in my back pants pocket. Apparently on the way home the book fell out of my pocket, which meant all the rations they were to receive were gone. My aunt never yelled at me in spite of what the horrible loss of those stamps was going to mean to their quality of life. From this I indirectly learned to control harsh feelings as much as possible especially over things that are not intentional. Obviously this was not the way most Italians are believed to react. Italians are stereotypically shown as extremely emotional and outspoken. I suppose there may be some truth to this image. I know I have deep personal emotions, but with the exception of a few times in my entire life, I cannot say my family was routinely prone to outbursts of anger.

What a joy on May 7, 1945 (V-E Day) and then later on August 15, 1945 (V-J Day) when victory was declared in Europe and Japan. Our town had a big celebration in the streets with people laughing, dancing, kissing and hugging. All those years of praying for the war to be over finally came to fruition, though President Truman declared September 2, 1945 as V-E Day when they had the formal signing of the surrender on board the USS Missouri in Tokyo Bay. Unfortunately the Korean War was close behind.

Chapter Two

Becoming a Jersey Girl

I grew up in the 1940's and 50's in the small town of Matawan, New Jersey. The name sounded similar to Mattewan in New Jersey where they had a mental institution and we would get teased about that. To be honest, I am not sure I could understand this unkind humor for those who must be institutionalized. We shrugged our shoulders and basically ignored the remarks. During the holidays the storeowners would have lighted Christmas trees on the sidewalks in front of the stores in the center of town. Famed television personality Ed Sullivan drove through the town one year and remarked in his newspaper column about the charming appearance of the town. We had two fresh water lakes to swim in and skate on in the winter when homeowners along the lake would pipe music over loud speakers for us to enjoy while skating. There were an abundance of country roads on which to ride our bikes. We lived a half an hour from the Jersey shore and an hour from New York City. School field trips took us to the fabulous museums in New York City and to see Broadway plays like *South Pacific* and *Where's Charlie* with Ray Bolger. Life was good. No one locked his or her door. I took painting, dance, and piano lessons and stayed in Girl Scouting from a Brownie Scout until I was a Senior Scout. I could walk to school from grammar school through high school and walk to most of my activities, unless I took a bus. We took a train to the roller skating rink where we danced couples dancing to organ music and wore fancy skating outfits and had our own shoe skates. No one had to transport me to any place. If a teacher or someone else's mother told us to do something, we did it. We knew darned well that if we went home complaining our parents would not take our side.

One day two big male bullies accosted my girlfriend and me as we were walking back from town. We must have been in about the fifth grade, and what they were attempting to do was quite inappropriate. We screamed, slapped, kicked and ran away to my girlfriend's house that was the closest and told her mother what happened. The next day my friend's mother saw the boys hanging around again. She went up to them and said, "You know, I heard that there are two big bullies that were trying to hurt my daughter and her friend. I would like to ask you if you would please protect the girls from them and be sure no one hurts them again." Well, I don't know what psychologists would say of this reverse psychology, but those two boys never bothered us again.

I met my husband at the age of 13 on a snowy day off from school when he washed my face with snow. The girls all knew that if you got tackled from behind and the guys pretended to wash your face with snow that they liked you. While we pretended to be angry, we secretly liked the whole thing. My girlfriends and I were stubborn, feisty and had no fear of competing against the boys in the playground, or in the classroom. Where society ever got the idea that girls in a classroom of boys would not perform is beyond me. I loved getting better grades and competing against them, and consequently we always were popular with the boys as well as other girls. Why I was different in this respect I can only speculate, but I do know that the men in my family and the fathers of my friends were not domineering, but loving and considerate. I know I learned to speak my mind at a very young age because they tell the story that when I was around four years old I was staying at an aunt's house. They tried to force me to eat spinach that they said was good for me. I got very annoyed and told my aunt and uncle, "You made it, you eat it." I secretly saw them laughing with their backs turned to me and then telling me that was not a nice thing to say. In my studies at Vermont College I found that men are drawn to tough women, and I know that is one feature my husband likes about me though I know I try his patience a lot.

We girls loved to play tackle football along with the boys until one day one of the mothers began to wonder about our motives. It was summer, and we were wearing short shorts and halter-tops. These thirteen-year-old boys did all they could to get the ball to us, so that we in turn could be tackled. That evening my friend's mother took us aside and kindly, but firmly, suggested that she thought we were getting a little old now to be playing tackle football with the boys, and it would be best if we found something better to fill our time. We knew she meant it, and I didn't need to ask my mother otherwise. At thirteen we stopped playing football. This worked out well because then I was entering high school, and I tried out for cheerleading. This would keep me active since they did not have sports for girls in those days, yet I do remember playing softball and basketball on the old half court. The guards had to stay on their half of the court while the forwards could travel the length of the entire court. Sometimes we did compete with other schools. I was also a cheerleader in college the one year I went away to Alfred University where I also played field hockey, basketball and volleyball. Being a cheerleader did not have the stigma against it that is prevalent today, nor were gymnastics involved. Cartwheels and high jumps were the most gymnastic things we did, along with synchronized formations. We would get kicked off the squad if we smoked, we had to maintain a good grade point average and have high moral standards. It was great for teaching me assertiveness and to get up before a crowd. The discipline required was good, and I went on to become a member of The National Honor Society. By the time I graduated from high school I received several scholarships for scholastic achievement and best all around personality.

New Jersey, as a state, often gets a bad rap, but for me it was a great place in which to grow. I can still name over a dozen of my teachers from grammar school and high school because they were excellent teachers, and they made a deep impression on me. I later met people from other parts of the country who were college educated, while I was not, but they never had studied a foreign language where I had two years of Latin and two years of French. I could also notice a huge difference in grammar skills, so I am grateful for the teachers that helped form my educational background.

The drive through Secaucus, New Jersey was part of the reason New Jersey got such a bad rap. There was an undeniably horrible odor from the former pig farms that were in close proximity as one drove by. The people of New Jersey knew however the benefits of the beautiful mountains, elegant ocean shoreline and the abundance of rivers and lakes for recreation – and all within a short driving distance. People that needed to judge our entire state by driving through one section could just keep right on driving where I was concerned. We didn't need them. That would be like driving through the devastated parts of the Bronx and calling all of New York City a dump. There were enough famous people living in our state who obviously would not have chosen to live there had it not been up to par. Jacqueline Kennedy had an estate in Short Hills, New Jersey for years where she would go to ride her horses. Some of our most famous actors, musicians and singers are from New Jersey, and many still choose to live there today. There is nothing like a good old Jersey tomato either. The state is not called the Garden State for nothing.

Chapter Three

Outside Influences

We spent a lot of time at the movie theater when we were young going to matinees and just congregating later at the soda shop. Movies definitely influenced us. Just as the young black children in Toni Morrison's novel *The Bluest Eye* wanted to have blue eyes and blonde hair, I wanted a nose like the actress Doris Day. She and Rock Hudson were two famous movie stars that had a series of love comedy films we enjoyed when I was of an impressionable age. Doris Day had what was called a cute "pug nose" and my nose was straight and called a Roman nose. I used to stand in front of the mirror trying to see how I would look if I changed my nose to a pug by lifting it up with my index finger. "Ugly" is the only word that comes to mind. One day, a very austere yet incongruously pleasant teacher from my grammar school who lived across the street from us stopped by the house for some reason. She looked at me and remarked that I had a beautiful straight Roman nose. She helped me to view this feature on my face with a whole new perspective. My nose became less of a concern and just something to use and appreciate for helping me to breathe.

The word teen suddenly became in vogue around the late 1940's. Magazines started to gear their advertisements to this young group of people, and we were given a category name all our own. I told my grandchildren I invented the words "going steady." My friends and I were joiners, and we belonged to just about any club in high school that would take us. I represented the Student Council, was a class officer multiple times, and was a certified school reporter with a press pass for the Asbury Park Press. I belonged to the Girls' Athletic Association (GAA). Diversification became the rule as I performed in school variety shows and had the lead in the senior play. Strange as it seems though I never remember family members coming to see me in any of these events like the senior play. I honestly cannot say if they were there or not.

My first real job was working at the local "5 & 10 cent store" when I was sixteen years old. The male boss had me using freezing cold water to wash candy tins that had once been filled with hard candy at a sink in the back of the store. I was hired to work the cash register and wait on people. One of the older women took me aside and said I did not have to do that type of work as that is not what I was hired to do. Had my boss asked me to do this again, after my conversation with the woman, I was prepared to refuse to do it. This was my first early lesson in not letting people take advantage of me in any way.

My boyfriend used to pick me up in his maroon Mustang with leopard seat covers. He lived around the block, and I could hear him "rev" up the motor. I would be ready when he got to my house. Along with my cousin, he raced stock cars at the local track. We spent time cheering for them in the stands. Unfortunately, we also watched them in some bad crashes. In the fall I went away to college in New York State.

Throughout high school, when I would be in a car full of boys that drove up in front of the house, my grandmother was right out there making sure I came directly inside. If I were leaving with boys in the car, she made sure they saw her. With our town being a small one those boys were not going to try a darn thing knowing my grandmother knew who was in the car.

Many young boys starting high school were trying so desperately to ask girls out on a date, but we found out that if we just went with the girls we could dance with a whole bunch of guys and not just the one date. It was so hard to turn them down as I hate to hurt anyone's feelings, but for one dance a boy named Carl asked if I would go with him. I gave him a vague excuse that I had promised my best girl friend I would go with her, but I would see him at the dance. Six more boys asked me to that same dance, but it got a little easier to refuse them by my telling each one, "I already turned down Carl, so it would not be fair to go with you, but thank you anyway." That evening, minutes before my girlfriend came across the street for us to leave who should come to pick me up but Carl. Apparently he did not understand my refusal. My girlfriend arrived right after him, and we all three stood there looking at each other. I mumbled something stupid, and off the three of us went to the dance. That whole night was awkward, but I learned my lesson to just come out and say no and not be overly conscious about hurting someone's feelings.

Chapter Four

Learning to Make Tough Choices

About the time I entered high school two very close male friends who lived on our block were killed in an automobile accident. The time was summer, and it was warm out. When I walked into that funeral parlor the smell of gardenias everywhere was overwhelming. I still can't smell gardenias today without thinking of funerals.

One warm sunny day in the late afternoon, soon after the funeral, my boyfriend and I were out for a drive in his fancy car on the many country roads that surrounded the area where I lived. There were no seatbelts in those days, and I could snuggle up to him closely while he put his arm around me as he steered the wheel with his other hand. We enjoyed smooching up a storm, and we became so enamored with each other the car drove off into a ditch on the side of the road. There was no way we could get the car out, and we were due home for dinner. Apparently, a farmer had watched the whole incident from his house and came to the rescue with a tractor, some rope and a sly smile on his face. Our parents looked equally strange when we walked in late for dinner with our slurred excuses and rumpled appearances.

Though I had been offered a scholarship to a college in Tennessee, my mother's oldest sister and her husband persuaded me to go to Alfred University in Alfred, New York. My uncle was from the town and graduated from Alfred with a degree in ceramic engineering. I was going to stay in their home near the campus. However, when I arrived on campus in the fall of 1951, my uncle got a job too good to turn down in Caracas, Venezuela, so I had the unexpected expense of staying in the dormitory and the out of state tuition. I was not able to return to Alfred University for my sophomore year. I had always planned to go to college and took the college preparatory course (as it was called then) in preparation while I was in high school. I had many teachers and family members pulling for me to complete this education, and the three to four monetary scholarships I received were proof that other organizations had high hopes for me as well. Therefore, when I made the tough choice not to return for my sophomore year, I was not only disappointed for myself, but also for the others who were rooting for me. I had the feeling I was letting down a lot of people. Money was indeed a big consideration, and I realized when my mother died a few years later that she was physically not able to continue to support my education. Many relatives had money, but we did not ask for nor discuss my situation with them. When they heard I was dropping out of school they felt those were my desires, and they let it go at that. Educating girls was not a big priority in those days. That summer I had a good paying job working for the federal government, so I chose to continue working there, and this certainly helped to assuage any concerns I had about not returning to school.

My boyfriend and I decided to marry at the age of nineteen years old. We were brought up to have good morals. If we wanted to be together, then getting married was pretty much the proper way to do that in the 1950's. Bill was working doing some type of drafting at a local business, so we were both making fairly good money. One Saturday afternoon while we were cleaning our apartment we overheard a commercial come on the television about dentistry. My husband said he had always thought he might like to be a dentist and without really much thought I said, "Well, why don't you look into it?" Those simple statements started us on a path that would lead to some marvelous adventures. There were no dental schools in our home state at that time, so he applied and was accepted to the University of Maryland.

As I explained earlier, we knew one of us needed to be educated. In those days it usually benefited everyone to have the male in the home educated because of prejudices against women in the employment world resulting in a lack of good pay and worthy positions. I was able to transfer my job with the government to the Office of the Chief Signal Officer at the Pentagon in Virginia (address Washington, DC) where I commuted by bus from our apartment in Maryland. I learned from my studies at Vermont College that women cannot always control the circumstances in their lives, but we could control what we chose to do about them. It became quite obvious that many of my choices were influenced by the time period in which I lived. The lack of birth control and the lack of high paying jobs for women were definite factors in my choosing to marry early, to have children at a young age, and to work for the government since they definitely gave better benefits than the average job for women. I loved the man I married, and I always dreamed of being a mother, so these were not hard choices for me to make. My great-grandfather used to say about my husband that he was a good worker and came from a line of good workers. That apparently was an Italian custom in my home where everyone was impressed by the work ethics of another. My great-grandfather did not say that about some of the other guys in my life. I sensed the importance of marrying someone with ambition, and marvel how this simple statement from a wise old man made such an impression on me. This was especially so since I was of an age where so many just want to defy any type of adult thoughts or actions. I often ponder why our reactions were so different from the youth of today. I began to realize that we had an unprecedented amount of freedom during the summer and after school. As long as we did not get into trouble, and came home when we were told, we were pretty much on our own. There is this freedom a child gets when they are not constantly being watched, ordered or stifled by adults. Because we were not pushed, we learned to respect. I know my family's rules were more stringent than those rules of other parents. The story used to be that if Lucille's family let her go to a function than the other parents felt it would be all right for their own children to go. Children and young adults today are very much more circumscribed and limited in what they are allowed to do. Consequently, they don't necessarily learn to fend for themselves in the ways that they should.

Chapter Five

Multiple War Years

So much of my life centered on wars being fought by our country. The Korean War was going strong by 1953, and while we had planned to marry in September of 1953, the draft board told my then boyfriend that he most likely would not be around in September, and he would be drafted into the service. So, we got married in July, and while we were on a cruise coming back from Bermuda they announced the Korean War was over. My husband quipped, "Oh, boy, now I've got a wife–and no war!" People did not attempt to plan their lives so much in advance as they do today in 2007. Many people today get their degrees, then they marry, wait a few years, and then they have children. There is a feeling they can control their lives. Somehow we sensed that all the planning in the world could be turned topsy-turvy in an instant, so we pretty much took things as they came. After all, we knew of families that had lost their life's savings in the depression years, we did not have birth control, borrowing money was not so easy to do, and we had multiple wars affecting our lives. I started having babies like they were going out of style which meant I no longer could work. We did not live near family, and we did not have day care centers. I did babysit for the children of the few wives who had only one child and who were able to work. This provided us with extra money.

My husband worked nearly forty hours a week at Johns Hopkins Hospital in Baltimore in addition to going to school. He worked at the hospital all night then went from there to school all day most days of the week. I used to pack him a grocery bag full of sandwiches to eat. To this day I still hate making sandwiches. Neither did we have health care which was something unavailable then. I had several miscarriages, and two came close together. We still owed the doctor a lot of money from the first miscarriage when I lost the second baby. I was alone, in the middle of the night, in a town house in Baltimore. I lost the baby while walking down the stairs to the one phone in the house to call my husband because of the severe pains I was suffering. After the call, I only had the energy to lie at the bottom of the stairs in a puddle of blood. Cell phones were not available then, and most people only had one house phone. My husband was across town, so he called my neighbor to ask her to come and stay with me until he could get home. Bill was told by the doctor to take me to the hospital. The doctor also told my husband that he would not treat me until our prior bill was paid. This was before credit cards and ATM's, and I don't know how my husband got the money unless someone wired it to him because we certainly did not have it in the bank. Some memories like that just draw blanks perhaps because they are just too difficult to remember.

When my husband finally graduated from dental school, we still had to be concerned about the military taking professionals into the service to treat the soldiers. If you set yourself up in private practice, borrowing thousands of dollars, you could stand to lose it all by being called into service, so most chose to go into the service right out of dental school and get the obligation out of the way. When we found out that they would train him to be a specialist, we decided together that my husband would stay in the service for a few more years. This ultimately turned out to be twenty-two years.

If you stayed in the service long enough in the sixties it was inevitable that you would be sent to Vietnam for a year, and my husband was no exception. I was left home alone for a whole year with four children, the youngest two years old. For months after my husband left, my two year old would point to a plane in the sky and say "Daddy's plane." I wonder what she thought Daddy was doing flying around for weeks at a time in the plane in the sky. This was during the time when the military did not have support groups for the spouses who remained behind. In my habit of always thinking things could be worse or other people probably had it worse (like the spouses of World Wars I and II who never knew when their men would be home), I did not feel sorry for myself. We had no e-mail. If we were lucky we got to talk a couple of times a year on a ham radio. The problem with the ham radio was that you had to say "over" every time you finished a sentence, and you could in no way get personal with your discussion because that ham radio operator sat there listening in on the whole conversation. In fact, one time I was trying to tell my husband softly that I loved him, and my husband could not hear me. I repeated it several times with several "overs," and finally the ham radio operator piped in and said, "She says she loves you Sir." I wrote my husband a letter every day, and I still have saved every letter he wrote to me though there are some parts I have blacked out with ink as just too personal.

We could send these little recording tapes, so one night I decided to bring the tape recorder to the kitchen table while the five of us were having dinner, and in that way my husband could have a little taste of home. That was the night the two year old decided to wear roller skates to the dinner table. Her older siblings did not like that at all. They were screaming and fighting and spilling milk, and I was getting more frustrated by the minute. Finally, I just decided to send the tape as it was – and oh yes, he really found out what he was missing by getting this little taste of home.

One morning I had the rare pleasure of sleeping a little later that usual when the jarring ring of the phone awoke me. It was a friend of my husband's who lived nearby who started the conversation with, "I am sure you don't have to worry about Bill, Lu, since he was most likely in a safe area." I was in a shocked daze and said, "What? Is there a problem?" He then said, "Oh, I am so sorry, did you not hear that the Viet Cong shelled your husband's base?" I was beside myself with fear. While I just sat in anguish, an aunt of mine who worked for a general at Fort Monmouth in New Jersey called and said her boss mentioned that he could see she was not going to be of any help to him until she found out about her nephew, so he offered to make some calls to see what he could find out. He arranged for her to actually talk with Bill and thank the good Lord he escaped injury. I was no more relieved however, since he flew frequently in Black Hawk helicopters, and a physician friend had recently been killed when one of those helicopters either crashed or was shot down. The Army was flying these professionals to the villages to actually do medical and dental work on the South Vietnamese. We have a video that was made from a 16mm reel of film that shows my husband working on these people with bullet holes on the wall in back of him.

There was a Dental Clinic at his camp location that was hardly completed when my husband got to Vietnam. He wrote me at home and asked me to purchase some weird sized special steel bolts that would be used to fix the overhead lights on the dental chairs. This was necessary so that the doctors could look inside their patients' mouths. When my husband left, I had made up my mind not to tell a lot of people he was away. Army spouses use to get prank phone calls from "sick" men mentioning suggestive sexual innuendos, and they used to know to call when the spouse was not yet home from work. I certainly did not need to deal with that on top of everything else, so I told only those closest to me that my husband was away. However, when I went to the hardware store to ask for the bolts, the men there looked at me so strangely and mentioned that the sizes were odd, and they wondered how I was going to use them. Remember that hardware stores in the 1960's were private stores with personalized help, and not big box stores like Home Depot. I finally had to mention why they were needed, and they actually were very accommodating after that.

The same thing happened with my septic tank. My husband had been stationed at Valley Forge General Hospital in Pennsylvania before going to Vietnam, and I remained near there when he was away. This was the only other general military hospital on the east coast next to Walter Reed Army Medical Center. Today, the Valley Forge Hospital is no longer operated by the military. We had a lot of snow in Pennsylvania the year my husband was away. Consequently, the septic tank kept filling and overflowing into the house. The stench was horrible and the clean up even worse. Finally, the guy who came out each time to empty the tank said to me, "Why don't you just have your husband block off the downstairs toilet, and then the runoff will not be able to enter your house." For the first time I cried, and the poor guy did not know what to do. I told him my husband was in Vietnam. He then felt so badly, he fixed it for me himself, and he didn't charge me a penny for the work. I use to jest later that if I had only known, I would have shed tears sooner. The tears were there, of course, when my husband left. In fact, it was the first time in about 17 years of marriage that I had ever seen tears in my husband's eyes.

My husband purposely bought me a new station wagon car so I would not be burdened with car troubles while he was away. The story used to say you got married, got a station wagon and a beer belly, and your wife was barefoot and pregnant. So, we fit the mold with the station wagon at least. The day we brought the new car home, I removed the gloves I had on only to look down and see that the diamond in my engagement ring was missing. There was nothing but a black hole where the diamond should be. I feared this was some kind of bad omen. Of course, many years later I have had more than my share of replacement diamonds. However, I can still feel the pit in my stomach the day I saw that black hole.

Well, the electronics were shot in the car, and I constantly had to take it for repairs miles from home while always having to make arrangements for someone to watch the children. Needless to say, we got used to knowing that no matter how much you plan in life, there are many obstacles along the way to upset the apple cart. My husband did end up receiving the Bronze Star and Legion of Merit Medals among many other prestigious medals. While the record books say we lost the Vietnam War, I am proud of my husband's service to his country during a very difficult and trying time in the lives of the citizens of America.

Chapter Six

Sources of Strength

My studies at Vermont College focused on many women who felt they were silenced in society by the men with whom they associated and perhaps by the way they were taught. I pondered what was different for me that I never felt silenced in any way. I met a young woman in her thirties at the community college I attended for a short time who was of Italian descent like I was. The class was having a tense discussion about sexuality and about the scenes that were depicted in some of the literature we had read. She remarked how her Italian mother brought suspicion, fear and old-fashioned ideas that seemed to hold this young woman back in the way her personality was shaped. Her mother was probably younger than I was, and I wondered how I escaped this in my life. After all, I was born when women were supposedly subservient to men. What made me different? I decided to examine my life to see what did make me different.

Remembering my childhood, I began to realize what a very simple, happy life it was. Sunday afternoons used to be spent driving around in the car with no particular destination in mind after enjoying a big meal with spaghetti and meatballs for sure. We had what they now call "pasta" and what we called macaroni at least two days out of the week. Pizza was not called pizza to me then either. It was called tomato pie, and the slices were not stiff enough to hold out as they are today. The slice was loaded with cheese that formed strings when you tried to chew it, and you would very often burn your mouth. There were no fast food restaurants in those days. We packed lunches and ate alongside the road wherever there happened to be picnic tables. In our young married years we continued taking these Sunday drives with our own family after church. Because of Blue Laws (Blue Laws got their name from the blue paper on which they were printed) that were mostly related to Sabbath observance closing stores on Sundays, we did not have the opportunity to go shopping. No stores were open on the weekends or in the evenings, but you did not miss what you never had.

We dressed up for everything. A female would never consider entering a church without a hat, mantilla, or some other covering on her head. We wore hose that had seams up the back leg, and it was so important to keep that seam going straight up the leg and not crooked. Pantyhose were not yet in style, so we had garter belts with little hooks that you attached to your hose that ended at the top of the thigh to hold up the stockings. We were the precursor to Victoria's Secret. What they now call sexy was normal for us, and more of a nuisance. We also wore Playtex rubber girdles because our skirts were so tight, and we didn't want anything to jiggle. Because of the tightness of those rubber girdles, once I moved to Hawaii and found the "muumuu" dress I never wore a girdle again, and today I won't wear the newer version called "spanx." No thank you Ma'am! When we wore sweaters, we wore the type of bra where we would be noticed. No pretense there. In many ways though we were covered from top to bottom with bobby sox and longer skirts, yet that didn't stop the guys with their ogling eyes. Perhaps the males felt as I did, that while we may have been on the cutting edge of sexuality for our day, a body that is fully exposed lacks a certain tantalizing sexuality that one gets when the body is seen peeking through a layer of covering. Nothing today is left to the imagination. Even our children were also dressed to the ultimate. The boys always had suits and white shirts and ties for church, and the girls had prissy little fancy dresses with patent leather Mary Jane shoes.

Easter Sundays were really special as we usually got new outfits from head to toe including fancy hats, hose, gloves and new shoes. The day always started out in church that morning. Our family used to go to the Easter Parade in Asbury Park, New Jersey in the afternoon and walk up and down the boardwalk where they had judges selecting the most beautiful outfits. I cannot imagine today walking on any boardwalk with high heels, but we certainly did it then. Our day was filled with eating cotton candy, people watching and the enticing salty aroma of the ocean air. Back home we still had baskets full of candy and fuzzy toy bunnies to enjoy. Hunting for the beautiful hard-boiled colored eggs was always fun. When we were newly married, we continued to spend a lot of time at Asbury Park's Convention Center dancing to the big bands that came there.

People often stopped by our home in the middle of the day. I loved listening to the women talk about politics, their vote in the election, the boss that they gave a piece of their mind, and the dress they brought back to one store because they found the same thing at another store for less money. I remember there was a risqué movie out, and I was walking in front of my mother and a lady friend. I was around ten years old. I overheard the friend ask my mother if she would let me see the movie. My mother said, "Of course. She is a good child and knows right from wrong, and I trust her judgment in seeing the movie." I began to see this pattern of strong women, the way they would talk back to the unruly boss and take part in town politics, and perhaps this is what gave me my strong assertive personality. These women were ahead of their time and were not burdened by old-fashioned ethnic rules. Some of my aunts attended business schools. Katherine Gibbs business school was quite prestigious for a girl to attend in those days. Most of the mothers of my friends worked outside the home, just like my own mother. Women worked in offices, factories, as nurses, and for the phone company. They owned hair salons and gift shops, and we knew everyone in the town from the librarian to the guys in the post office. When I lived in Hawaii, if I got packages in the mail, a high school friend who worked in the post office used to write me notes on the outer wrap of the package. I knew of no female doctors when I was young, nor of any female executives, though many females I knew owned shops. More and more women were going to college when I was entering my teens, and things were clearly moving in the direction of greater equality as far as my own family and home life were concerned. While women were not yet entering male dominated professions in large numbers, the women in my life were definitely confident about pushing the envelope in terms of working outside the home and going to school.

The Italian men I knew were loving and compassionate. They helped cook good meals and treated the women with respect. Mafia was a word I only began to hear once the Godfather movies came out. I never once saw a gun in anyone's house until I was much older and met my non-Italian father-in-law who was a hunter. It was not uncommon for both the men and the women to discuss politics around the dinner table in my grandparent's home. I loved those discussions. We had members of both political parties represented in my household, so I have always voted for the person I thought was the most capable to be running a country at any given time. When I read the book *From Paesani to White Ethnics: The Italian Experience in Philadelphia* by Stefano Luconi, I found that it was common practice for Italians to vote for both the Republicans and the Democrats depending on the politics of the time period.

Sometimes because I lived away and had to vote by absentee ballot ahead of time, something might have occurred to make me change my mind on my vote, but there was nothing I could do about it. I liked the fact that my family was not completely one way or the other when they voted. I am often concerned about people who don't consider the issues, but who tend to vote only along party lines all their lives.

Chapter Seven

Italian Americanness

The family often spoke Italian. While I could understand most things they said I could never speak Italian, and I thought that was odd. The oddity did not really impress me until I was an adult. I must assume that it did not really matter to me if I could speak Italian or not as a child. When my family did speak Italian I became fascinated as I tried to figure out by their intonations when something was good or bad, funny or sad. When one blurted out an Italian swear word, of which I quickly learned the meaning, it was easy to tell because the others would at first gasp and then giggle. None of my friends spoke a foreign language, so I imagine that since my mother and aunts spoke only English to me I just went along with the crowd. My grandparents did have an accent as did my great-grandfather, and his daughter (my great aunt) criticized him for his accent and sometimes did not want him around certain people. To make matters worse, none of my friends had grandparents living with them, so I did not hear accents in their home. My aunt's beliefs only perpetuated my own insecurities, and I would get embarrassed when my friends first heard my grandparents speak with their accent. Ethnicity when I was a child was not as treasured as it is today as Italians and other immigrants tried to assimilate into American society. Italian friends my age who lived in tight knit Italian communities did not speak Italian either. When I lived in Germany I did not expect the Germans to learn my language to converse with me, and contrary to popular belief not all foreigners speak English. I found from experience that even if they do speak English they are not always willing to use it when speaking with Americans. Knowing today how our ethnicity was not as treasured when I was a child has perhaps made me unusually willing to go out of my way to accommodate others' language and culture when I was traveling – e.g. when I was in Germany. Had I remained in Germany, I would have tried very hard to study the German language.

My great-grandfather lived to be ninety-seven years old and used to climb up our steep stairs to the bathroom using both his hands and feet. I would lie in bed cringing until I knew he was safely up or down. A retired railroad employee, he used to love to work on a strawberry farm picking strawberries well into his eighties. A truck loaded with young children workers would come to pick him up every day and bring him home. One day he came home with a thorn in his eyeball. It was horrible to see and the family was frightened. They took him to the doctor, and he was told not to return to work. The family told the truck driver not to stop by to pick him up anymore. So what did my grandfather do? In his eighties, he walked over two miles in the hot summer sun to go and continue to pick strawberries. The family had no idea where he had gone until he rode home on the truck later that day.

Another time he was sitting in a rocker on our front porch. Sitting on the front porch was a delight to everyone in the family, and we often played jacks on the front porch too. This particular evening I was across the street at my girlfriend's house. I called my home on the phone wanting to ask my mother if I could go to the movies. I could hear the phone ring from across the street, and I saw my grandfather get up. I didn't know he was home alone. He answered the phone and I said, "Grandpa, this is Lucille, may I please talk to my mother?"

He replied, "Lucilla, she's a no home."

I said, "No grandpa, this is Lucille."

Again he says "Lucilla, she's a no home," then he hesitated and said, "Wait a minuto." He goes to the front door and calls across the street for me. I had to hang up the phone I was on, go home and take the other phone, and I had to pretend I was talking to someone. He always gave us a good laugh.

Much was made of our family being related to Philip Mazzei (1730-1816) who was a Florentine merchant, surgeon, horticulturist and a good friend of Thomas Jefferson. I never really paid much attention to the details, and now I wish I had done so. I do know we were given a book about his life by a society of nuns who were doing research on Philip Mazzei and his descendants. We also have a commemorative stamp in his honor. I could not help but notice just what a good friend he was to President Jefferson when I went to Jefferson's home in Monticello, Virginia and could actually see Mr. Mazzei's wife had been buried in the Jefferson family cemetery. My mother's maiden name is Mazzei and her father was Rocco Mazzei. Some families would be making much to do over this type of relationship, but I never got that impression from my own family except hearing about the meetings with the nuns and how they use to come back and say how impressed they were by how well the women that were their age could speak such fluent Italian. While my elders all spoke Italian as well as English, they did not think their Italian was eloquent enough. Their English speaking skills I can heartily vouch for which were indeed eloquent. Fillipo Mazzei was featured in a book *Closet Italians: A Dazzling Collection of Illustrious Italians with Non Italian Names* written by Nick J. Mileti. The author wrote, "Who wouldn't love the man who originally wrote the words that his friend Thomas Jefferson paraphrased in the Declaration of Independence: 'We hold these truths to be self-evident. That all men are created equal, that they are endowed by their Creator with certain inalienable Rights.'" (Mileti 2004).

A book *The History of Monmouth County, New Jersey 1664-1920* edited by Frank R. Holmes was published with the biographies of our townsfolk who had made an impression in their personal lives and in the business community. A cousin of mine gave me a paper copy of the page that featured this writing about my grandfather, "He had completed his education in the public schools in Cavello, Italy and entered the shoe business. Subsequently, he established himself in the shoe business in Matawan, New Jersey, after coming to the United States in 1903." The article claims "he was a self-made man who came to the country poor in finances, but rich in shrewdness and foresight, traits which go to make up the successful man. He has always been found among the loyal supporters of progressive movements for his community's welfare, and when opportunity has offered he has been ready to aid those less fortunate than himself." (Holmes 1922). These wonderful traits have filtered down among his descendants.

I learned more about my grandfather's background from the research of sociologist Herbert Gans who mentioned that in many towns in Italy schools were run largely for the children of higher classes, so again since my grandfather was privileged to attend school, it would be safe to conclude that he was not as desperately poor as many who came to America. Plus, he was an "artigiano" or artisan who included craftsmen and small shopkeepers who Gans said enjoyed a higher standard of living. I do not believe my grandparents had an arranged marriage either as did many early immigrants because I do remember some of my grandmother's tales while we were sitting on the beach in Hawaii. She told of my grandfather's pursuit of her after they came to this country and while living in Jersey City, New Jersey. The first time my grandmother flew on a plane was when she came to Hawaii to visit me along with her son and daughter-in-law. She flew on a big 747 plane and stood at the bar, and I was told she was the "hit" of everyone on the plane. There was a lot of industrial violence in Italy during the years 1878 to 1903 (the year my grandfather arrived in America), and this could easily have been one of the reasons he chose to come to this country.

My paternal grandfather owned a combination barbershop and beauty parlor where most of his children worked. They lived over the business in a large apartment on the Jersey Shore in Bradley Beach, New Jersey. My grandfather owned the entire block long building that housed other businesses, and he also purchased other property in the area. This same building is still owned by remaining family members. My lovely petite, blue-eyed grandmother always brought out the good China when inviting us to dinner, so it was apparent that there was not a lot of animosity between family members where my parents' separation was concerned. These grandparents came from the Naples area of Italy to America with my father, their two-year-old son, in the year 1907. They were married at the ages of nineteen and seventeen years old. Most of their children were in their late twenties when they eventually married. They had eleven living children by the time they died. My father (also a barber with his own business) was the oldest, but he died at the youngest age. The youngest of the eleven is my Aunt Gloria, and we are the best of relatives and friends. We still today keep in frequent contact. She tells me how my father played the mandolin in his barbershop and was also a volunteer fireman. When the siren would blow, and he was in the middle of cutting someone's hair, he would leave the customer sitting in the chair while he went to the fire. Apparently, they loved his ebullient personality, always with a smile on his face, singing and happy, and they were willing to tolerate this inconvenience. Many of the other siblings are talented musicians playing in bands and writing published songs. I can see I inherited a lot of my tastes and talents from this side of the family too.

My grandfather Mazzei died a month before my wedding on Father's Day. He was like my own father, and he had been ill with diabetes. Those weeks before he died, whenever I got a phone call at work, I picked it up with fear of what type of news I would get. I could not even walk down the street and see an elderly man without thinking of my grandfather and wanting to burst out into tears. They put the casket in the living room of our home for several days, and people and flowers were all over the place. My grandmother donned black clothing on the day he died and wore black for a full year after his death which meant she also wore black to my wedding. My grandfather had already told me he could not walk me down the aisle before he died. I chose instead one of my favorite uncles who had no children as he might never otherwise get the opportunity to walk anyone down the aisle. His wife was so overcome by this gesture she could not even go inside the church to see the wedding. This particular uncle was my grandmother's brother, so he was my great-uncle, and his wife was my father's sister, so I was related to both of them before they ever got married to each other. We had our reception at the beautiful Molly Pitcher Hotel in Red Bank, New Jersey which is still in business today, but because of my grandfather's death we were not allowed to have any music at the wedding reception. This apparently was a transition time for these then traditional customs because only a few years later the dead were laid out at a funeral parlor and widows stopped wearing black for a full year. Today, people party with music almost immediately after a funeral. I personally am very happy with the changes in these customs. I believe in showing respect while people are living and to not prolong the burying of the dead. Psychologically, I feel we are better off not dwelling on the mourning process and we should attempt to get on with life while we can.

New Year's Eve was always a big time at our home (the home of my grandparents). People just dropped in from all over town that night, and we would have sixty or more guests yearly. There would be game tables, poker playing, dancing in the living room and food galore. One year my uncle dressed up like "Old Man Time" and my young son in his diaper was baby "New Year." Everyone would hug and kiss at midnight. As each generation got older, they would leave to go to their own group parties, but often the next few years they would be back. No party was as much fun as the one at home. I am sure the Italian American's love of family is part of the reason we kept going back. There is a simple comfort of being around loved ones that one does not experience in a nightclub or other fancy place full of strangers. I say this from experience as I too experimented with group parties before going back to be with family in the following years. Years later, we carried on the custom in my own home after I moved away with my children and their families.

Sometimes in life families assimilate and change customs because they are forward thinking and learn a better way to do things. When a custom is worth continuing, like socializing together at holiday dinners, then these customs are continued, but even they change as was noted when we served the traditional American turkey dinner along with the added addition of abundant Italian foods. Some ethnic groups assimilate to a new country faster than others because they move into new neighborhoods with a variety of different groups of people. For example, author Herbert Gans explained in his book *The Urban Villagers: Group and Class in the Life of Italian Americans* how most of the businesses owned in the West End of Boston were owned or managed by people who lived in the West End, and who were socially and culturally like their customers. Mr. Gans even goes on to say that "West Enders' detachment from the larger society has been supported by ethnic differences between themselves and the outside world." (Gans 1982). Those Italians in the West End would not be as inclined to want to form new customs, nor to assimilate. They were quite comfortable associating with their own peers. Mr. Stefano

Luconi stated, "Italian immigrants to Philadelphia tended to cluster together along regional, provincial, or even village lines in separate but overcrowded neighborhoods within the broader Italian settlements." (Luconi 2001). In the case of my family, once they experienced a new environment outside the Italian community, they assimilated and carried on the traditions that made them happy and set aside those traditions that were too depressing to continue.

Chapter Eight

My Transient Life

So much of my married life was shaped by the experience of being a military wife. I have a plaque on my wall that aptly depicts what it takes to be a military spouse to the "nth" degree. The author is anonymous, but the recipe goes like this:

> *Recipe for a Military Wife*
> *1-1/2 C. patience—3/4 C. tolerance—1 lb. Courage— dash of adventure*
> *With above ingredients, add 2 tsp. Elbow grease. Let sit alone 1 year. Marinate frequently with salty tears. Pour off excess fat. Sprinkle ever so lightly with money. "Knead" dough 'til payday. Season with international spices. Bake 20 years or until done. Serve with pride.*

I had four healthy children and four miscarriages. After my husband graduated from school in Maryland we lived for a year in Colonie, New York and then moved to Jersey and from New Jersey, to El Paso, Texas. Then it was back to Jersey for a year and on to Pennsylvania for four years. One of those four years my husband was in Vietnam. From Pennsylvania we went to Hawaii and then to Oklahoma. What a culture shock that was. We went from eighty-five-degree temperatures year round to 115 degrees the day we arrived in Lawton, Oklahoma. We went from flip-flops to cowboy boots, from serene weather to tornadoes. Never had I lived in a place where the natives were fearful of the weather though we did have a serious weather related incident in New Jersey when I was in high school. There was a horrible hurricane, and it tore down the chimney on the roof of our home. The bricks fell down inside the chimney near the furnace causing a blockage problem. Around the time we usually were to awaken our home was filled with carbon monoxide gas. Fortunately, we did awaken, but all of us were extremely nauseous and had to leave the house. Had this happened on a different time schedule they said we probably all would have been dead.

In Oklahoma, instead of things being opened and airy, everything was closed, dark and air-conditioned. I started to get panic attacks. The whole four years we lived in Hawaii I did not get home to see any family though some did visit us. While I was back on the mainland in Oklahoma, I still was not close to home. As a military wife you learn to adjust, and we bought a lovely new home in Oklahoma, and we put in a pool to cover those extremely hot days. I missed being near an ocean while living in the middle of the country.

My husband was offered the opportunity to go to the Command and General Staff College in Kansas. This was the route to take to become a General in the Army. Most people offered this opportunity would not have turned it down. My husband did turn it down though after discussing it with me. We just could not see our children, at the ages that they were at the time, having to pick up and move for just one year. Being a General would have meant more administrative work. My husband had not trained all those years doing dentistry to give it up at this point. He was a specialist now and it somehow seemed like it would have been a waste of all that additional education and training. After four years in Oklahoma my husband was transferred to Walter Reed Army Medical Center in Washington, DC. Finally we were going to be back east near family.

For so many years I was an active Army wife belonging to the Officer's Wives' Club, PTA at all the schools where we lived, and did a multitude of volunteer work. I spent hours attending all my children's activities from football, to baseball, to dance lessons, Homecoming festivities, hula lessons, swimming lessons, piano lessons, scouting, surfing, diving and wrestling competitions. They excelled, and my husband and I were proud parents. Society was changing in the 1960's and 1970's, and more women were starting once again to work outside the home. You almost began to feel strange saying you stayed at home, and women attempted making up pleasant names like "domestic engineer" instead of "housewife" or "homemaker" when the inevitable question would come up at cocktail parties as to what you did. Military life was very social and we had parties in the homes and officers' clubs wherever we lived. We belonged to bowling leagues, bridge groups, discussion groups, and traveled to marvelous places.

In the later years the military started getting paid twice a month, but most of the time my husband was in the service we got paid once a month. As I said earlier, there were no ATM's or credit cards to buy groceries. If you ran out of money before the end of the month, that was it – you were out of money. I learned to buy at the first of the month some roasts, hams and fancy food to freeze for the month in case company came. That way I knew I could always feed them. I came from a household with an abundance of food, and I needed to be prepared. During the middle of the month I could make any variations of Spanish rice, pasta, tuna casseroles, and hamburger meals and hot dogs, and if we didn't get company during that time we ate big at the end of the month. Once my father-in-law went fishing and caught a huge tuna that he gave to us. We thought we had died and gone to heaven. We had tuna casserole, baked tuna, tuna salad, tuna everything for over a week.

The budget was also a factor when we would get unexpected company while living in some new and different place. My quite elderly grandmother and her equally elderly sister decided to come visit us in El Paso, Texas around 1964. El Paso was our first assignment in the military. My husband had to leave six weeks before me, so I boarded the plane with the three children we had at the time. I hate flying and had flown only once on our honeymoon. This seems odd to say since I have now flown all over the world on 747's, Air Buses, military transports like the C5A and C130 and even a small six to eight passenger plane and a helicopter flight over New York City (a treat from my son). I have also flown in a hot air balloon. What put me at ease the day I flew to El Paso with my three children was when the renowned Archbishop Fulton Sheen, esteemed author and television personality, boarded our plane. Everything about him and his appearance put me immediately at ease as he sat near us. But, I digress.

My two elderly relatives came by bus to El Paso from New Jersey, and they decided they wanted to go to Las Vegas because when you looked on the map Las Vegas was a lot closer to El Paso than New Jersey. Right! My husband and I had to take out a loan from Household Finance to help make the trip. Everyone thinks since you are a professional and an Army Officer to boot that you are loaded. No one realized our educational debts and once a month salary. Off we went with our borrowed money in a five passenger Vintage Rose Thunderbird – our first big monetary splurge, and one that in reality was too small for our family. It had bucket seats in the front where two people sat and two seats in the back where two adults sat each with an either five, seven or ten year old on their lap and one child straddling the hump in the middle. Seatbelts were not a requirement at the time. When we stayed overnight in Phoenix, the room they gave us was far from the pool, and my aunt requested a room near the pool. The person at the registration desk had an odd smile on her face and said, "Oh, if you request this room we will definitely give it to you." During the night we heard this horrendous roar and could see a bright light coming right at us through the window getting closer and closer and the noise got louder and louder, and we realized it was a train, and we all screamed and sat up in our beds. The way the track curved right parallel to our motel room it appeared as though we were directly in the path of the train. We did go on to have a fun trip, singing in the crowded car, and the older women enjoying the slots. There was no gambling in Atlantic City at that time.

If the military life taught me anything at all besides being a strong woman it was to adjust to the unusual and to essentially be a good actress. Just when you would get settled in a home and the last curtain was hung, it was time to pick up and move again to a strange new place where most of the time you knew no one else. So, you adjusted by putting yourself out there and meeting new friends. You also learned how people are different all over the world and you accepted them for their differences. You became a good actress by always pretending to be brave because you had a family, and you wanted them to know everything would be fine when it sometimes was not all right. You grew up fast without having family members around for support in times of crises. Many times you had to do things even without the help of a spouse who got sent to strange places around the world. Sometimes, through hardship, you discover confidence, imagination, creativity and assertiveness. All of these qualities helped make me the person I ultimately became. I have many friends who were military spouses. We have a special bond from sharing our unique experiences. These experiences we would not trade with anyone.

Chapter Nine

Being a Woman

I was impressed by a statement that did not fit my life at all. Carolyn G. Heilbrun wrote in her book *Writing a Woman's Life* "We women have lived too much with closure: If he notices me, if I marry him, if I get into college, if I get this work accepted, if I get that job—there always seems to loom the possibility of something being over, settled, sweeping clear the way for contentment." (Heilbrun 1988). I always knew I wanted to marry the man I married and from there things just happened. When my mother died at the age of forty-four years, I learned to enjoy each day for what it gave me, and things just sort of occurred. I did not "if" my life away at all.

Perhaps I did not "if" my life away because we did not have things like the pill, or FASFA loans, or we experienced many wars that caused us to feel we did not know what tomorrow might bring, so we made the best use of the present. People today try to control everything. They say we will get married at a certain age and have a child two years after. They don't have that special feeling I always had that the apple cart could upset at any moment. Perhaps this is because I experienced the loss of my father at such a young age. I also have a belief in a divine being who I feel has the ultimate control over us. So, I bucked the trend of "iffing" my life by taking advantage of opportunities as they came and making the most of each opportunity. I also did not have a commitment phobia that I see so very prevalent among today's young adults. I was in love and got married, simple as that. However, I would be the first to say do not get married just for the sake of being married. You do not need another individual to validate yourself.

I worked for the federal government at Fort Monmouth, New Jersey in the enlistment office, and later at the Pentagon in Washington, D.C. in the office of the Chief Signal Officer in the 1950's. In the 1960's in El Paso, Texas, I continued my work with the federal government working on the schedules of the foreign students in attendance at the training school there. My return to the working world was an example of how my life was shaped by an opportunity for which I had not planned that took place sixteen years after my last child was born. I was not really looking for a job, but my oldest daughter was home for the summer from college, and she was looking for a job. I went along with her to wait because we were going to go shopping after. The secretary thought we were both applying and gave me the paperwork to take a test along with my daughter. I was too embarrassed to tell her at that point I was just waiting, so I thought well why not take the test as it will kill time. Because I was not nervous about taking a test since what did it matter if I failed, I finished rather promptly, and apparently they liked what I did because I was hired on the spot. Then, I really felt like a jerk to tell her I was not seriously considering working, so I said when she told me to come in the following Monday that maybe it would not work out because I had to take two weeks off in a few weeks to go to my son's college graduation out of state. They said, "We will work around that." I stayed in that job at Sears, Roebuck and Company for three years until we moved to Europe. My daughter did not get the job because they knew she was going back to college and they wanted a permanent employee.

My intentions were hopefully again to go to work for the federal government in Europe when my husband was sent in 1983 to command a Dentac Unit that encompassed the entire Bavarian region of Germany. However, I ran into a most unusual prejudice. Prior to the 1980's, spouses of military officer personnel primarily did not hold jobs outside the home, but this was changing fast. When you work for the government you do have priority in job status once you attain a career appointment which I had done. In most cases, you could equal the amount of money you had made in your last job, but very often your grade level was dropped dramatically. I had to take what jobs were available, and that usually meant a much lower grade which was really damaging to any promotion potential in my government career. It would have been the same in the civilian community as well.

My husband left for Nuremberg, Germany six weeks before me while I got my youngest child settled in college. Here again I was living life in reverse. When the last child leaves home the mother usually experiences the "empty nest" syndrome. In this case, I was the one that was leaving my baby behind, and it felt lousy. Furthermore, we left our home with everything in it to be lived in by my son and his wife. My son was setting up his own dental practice. As a Commander, my husband would be given a lovely home for us to stay in, but what most could not comprehend was that we were still paying a mortgage payment for our home in Maryland. His paycheck was suddenly reduced because we no longer were getting the cost of living pay in his check to compensate for the expense of living in the Washington, DC area. This time I was going back to work because my income was needed. The wife of the Deputy Commander who was taking our place until we arrived told me I should not expect to work. It was not proper for a Commander's wife to hold a job. Well, I won't print here what I would have liked to have told her. I did say to her however, "Well, this Commander's wife 'is' going to work," and I did. How odd though that no one seemed to question a divorced General also assigned to our area, who had recently remarried someone young enough to be his daughter. She was also a working wife. Prejudice was all around me.

Opportunities for women were slow in opening up in the 1980's in some segments of society. The military mindset expected spouses to remain at home and keep the home fires burning, and definitely did not include working outside the home. They expected you to be available to attend a myriad of activities and Wives' Club functions. Eventually, enough younger women arrived who preferred to work and were not interested in Wives' Clubs, but I was caught in the middle with my advancing age and the presumption that a high ranking officer could afford to support his wife without her working outside the home. Had I been a military nurse however, married to a military doctor, that would have been perfectly acceptable. The military culture is gradually opening up more working opportunities for women in society though perhaps at a slower and more uneven pace. Civil service jobs for women working for the government were more advanced for years, but moving around a lot following a military spouse was a detriment to career advancement in most cases. When you work for the government you do have priority in job status once you attain a career appointment which I did at the Pentagon while working for the Chief Signal Officer.

In addition to my job in Europe, I was expected to assume a whole new set of duties as the wife of the Dentac Commander. I was the advisor to a huge group of military spouses in the Bavarian region of Germany. I gave lectures and presentations at Wives' Club Meetings and at seminars. I was not a public speaker and I had no training. Most of the women I spoke to were better educated than I was (though most of them did not know this). Again you can see the life lived in reverse syndrome. Many public speakers go to college or take special courses in public speaking before they lecture to the public. I was just thrown into the situation. I was also the Advisor to the Health Services Auxiliary. This group investigated all medical complaints among doctors and patients, and we organized a system to facilitate the patient wanting to file a complaint. One reason I was so willing to take on these extra burdens, besides holding a full time job, was that my husband never once told me I had to do any of it. He was a maverick soldier and supported me always in my decisions. Somehow though, the more he spoke up for what he thought was justice, without fear of being demoted or thrown out of service, the more promotions he got. Perhaps for men too, strength, fortitude and assertiveness are as important as they are for women.

The Deputy's wife, and the other women, told my husband to be sure and let them know when I arrived in Europe as they wanted to meet me. However, the day I arrived, my husband got me out of town and we went to the Octoberfest (a German beer festival) in Munich, Germany, and we enjoyed being alone for a few days. So, it was nearly a week after I arrived in Germany before I called the women. I wish you could have heard them when they realized I had been there for a week already. "Oh," they said, "isn't he something, just taking you away and not letting us know you were here." At the Fest I stopped to go to the ladies room and came out and told my husband I needed one Mark to deposit for use in the stall. He said, "You've got to be kidding." Then he laughed and realized I only needed one Pfenning with the Mark being worth a lot more money. I obviously had a lot to learn in addition to taking the International Driving Test for my driver's license. I loved getting on the autobahns and just speeding away. I learned quickly when someone blinked his/her lights behind me to swiftly move over to the right.

Throughout my entire career I worked a lot with numbers. I was a Property Book Manager and prepared forty-two monthly Equipment Readiness Reports which meant coordinating my work with thirty other team managers. Keeping track of humvees, tanks and other armored equipment all over Europe was a huge responsibility. Mistakes were not tolerated, and it involved working with a lot of numbers. I then transferred to the Nuremberg Army Hospital Emergency Room Department. In addition to triaging patients and transcribing physicians' orders, I ordered and maintained stock levels for all ER forms and general office supplies. I compiled the statistics and prepared the end-of-month morbidity and medical summary reports and assisted with the monthly manpower reports. For this I won a large monetary award for my ideas on helping to reorganize the ER into a more efficiently run facility. I mention all of this because I obviously worked with a lot of numbers. In addition, I handled the household budget since my husband had gone to Vietnam, and we paid off all his educational debts and paid our mortgage off thirteen years early. Yet, when I wanted to go back to college they expected me to take a traditional math course. I hated advanced math since high school when I had a teacher who terrified me in the classroom by calling me abruptly by my last name which was totally inappropriate for the time period. That was why returning to Vermont College was so great. I got my math requirement out of the way the first semester – statistics, no less, and my professor Sue Cobb made it fun.

There have been many harassment laws put on the books since I worked and for very good reasons. In my experience, some men could be very crude, rude and obnoxious when I was working where women were concerned. They would call us Tiger, Babe, Cutie, you name it and just walking by them you wanted to crawl in a hole because of the remarks, whistles and sexual innuendoes they would make. These men were out of control, and there was neither rule nor person that could stop them. If you wore a dress with a belt that accentuated your waist they would say things like, "You look so lovely, that dress brings out your inner beauty." A simple "you look very nice today" would have been sufficient. There were no laws to protect against abusive behavior or actions. We could ignore, retaliate, or put up with it. Probably at one time or another I applied all of those techniques. Because I was a friendly person, there is a tendency for individuals to think at first they could push my buttons, but when they saw I could quickly turn off my friendliness by my manner and attitude they immediately realized they had better stop what they would be doing as they could tell I would make trouble. I did find that if individuals worked in close proximity to me, and they found out that I indeed was a lady, they ultimately would back off and learn to treat me with respect. I would not have been able to file any grievances because there were no grievances for us to file. If one had a disability, you most likely would have had to quit your job. However, having the laws on the books is not always a deterrent either. Some men like to harass females even today knowing what the consequences might be. We have only to remember the 1991 Tailhook scandal in which many Navy personnel were accused of sexual harassment and misconduct to know that there is still a lot of male domination in the military. Civilian males working for the government and those in private enterprise can be equally as bad.

We took advantage of this assignment in Germany to travel all over Europe, the Middle East, Asia and Africa, to name some destinations.

Lucille's parents wedding picture.

Bill's parents.

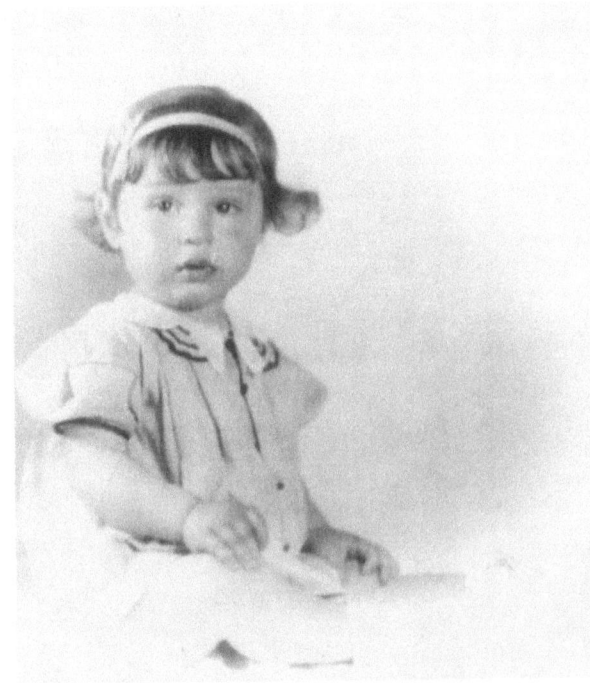

Lucille's Baby Picture.

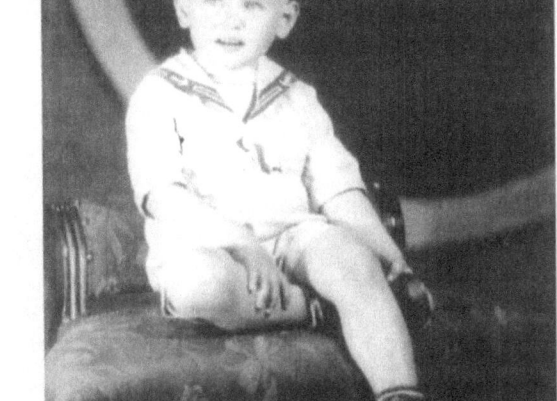

Bill's Baby Picture.

Lucille at 13 years of age when she met Bill-1949.

Bill at 13 years of age when he met Lucille-1949.

8th Grade Class Trip to Philadelphia–Notice how dressed up the girls are–Lucille in middle with dark hair-1948.

Lucille–High School Cheerleader-1951.

Bill on the High School Football Team-1951.

Lucille and Bill's Wedding Photo—July 19, 1953.

Bill and Baby Gary in front of Christmas tree with the perfect hanging tinsel–1958.

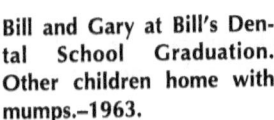

Bill and Gary at Bill's Dental School Graduation. Other children home with mumps.–1963.

Bill in Vietnam–1969.

Lucille and daughter Sandy ice skating on their pool in Oklahoma-1978.

Bill hooding our son Gary at Gary's Dental School Graduation—May 1983.

Daughter Pam's wedding at the US Naval Academy wearing Lucille's wedding gown–1983.

Lucille riding a camel in Israel-1984.

Lucille near the Sphinx and Pyramids in Egypt-1984.

Lucille and granddaughters in Corolla, North Carolina in hot tub–1993.

Grandchildren eating at the beach–1993.

Male relatives serenading Lucille's Grandmother at her 100th birthday to the tune of "Oh you Beautiful Doll."–1987.

On the ferry to Ellis Island with son Greg and children –Twin Towers in Background- 1999.

Lucille receiving award from the Military-1986.

Jheremy and Lucille gazed at by Jheremy's daughter-2007.

Surfing Grandchildren in Ocean City, Maryland–2003.

Lucille, Bill and their four children on a beach in Delaware–1996.

The twelve grandchildren at the beach in Delaware-1996.

Lucille's whole family and mother-in-law Catherine at the beach–1996.

Bill parasailing on his 55th Wedding Anniversary over Ocean City, MD-2008.

Lucille parasailing with her daughter-in-law Sarah on Lucille's 55th

Chapter Ten

Living the Good Life

After my spouse retired from the military, we moved back to Maryland once again. My husband worked as a Professor at the University of Maryland Dental School, and he worked in his son's dental practice as a specialist part time. Prior to moving back to the States, Bill took some additional training in implant dentistry at the University in Gutenberg, Sweden. I also worked for my son and did a lot of babysitting as now all my children were married and grandbabies were abundant. I helped my daughter establish a day care center and had done the same while stationed in Oklahoma. This was just a wonderful time being a grandmother at only forty-eight years of age. At this point I would not have traded my life for any other way imaginable. Every year, for more years than I can remember our family went to the beach in Ocean City, Maryland for a week and sometimes to Duck or Corolla, North Carolina. Everyone that could make it did make it. We kept renting more space as fiancées came, then new sons-in-law, or new daughters-in-law, and then the babies. We also purchased our own vacation condo in Ocean City, Maryland. We continue to visit all of these vacation places at the beach today.

Before my husband fully retired from all his other jobs, and implants in the dental field were becoming the thing to do, we were well on our way to becoming extremely wealthy. His practice grew tremendously, and many of our friends in the same situation were buying bigger and better homes. My husband began to have eyesight trouble doing such close detailed work, and he hated charging people all that money. During his Army career he just could treat the patient without worrying about money. The tension got to be too much, and he was ready to retire. That was one of the easiest decisions we ever made. Money is fine, and so is luxury, but we were living a good life regardless. We didn't need more, and our retirement years have been some of the best.

Returning from Europe was the perfect time to live this aforementioned good life. I enjoyed going to New York City to see plays and live television. I was on a special segment on Live with Regis and Kathie Lee (before Kelly Ripa) one year, getting my fifteen minutes of fame with the Amazing Kreskin. I assisted him while he utilized his magic powers to find a check that had been hidden outside the studio. Friends saw me from all over the country, and it was fun receiving letters and phone calls.

Often we got to meet famous people just by being in the right place at the right time. One day my husband and I had decided to take the Metro into Washington, DC to see the cherry blossoms and enjoy a casual afternoon. We packed backpacks with a lunch, and we stopped by the Jefferson Memorial to eat on the steps when we saw all this commotion and security personnel. This was before 9/11 when security was not that obvious. We overheard someone famous was coming as it was Thomas Jefferson's birthday. There was to be a special celebration. A man dressed like Thomas Jefferson appeared, and we went through a security checkpoint. We figured we might as well get in on the fun. Sure enough, soon after President Bill Clinton and his wife Hillary arrived. We got to shake their hands. One time I went to a football game at the University of Maryland and Queen Elizabeth was there at the game riding around in a limo for all of us to see. I believe it was her first time at a football game ever. Then, in Hawaii, we were out for one of our Sunday drives and saw a polo match, so decided to stop and watch. Who was there that day playing polo, but Prince Charles. We went to see Pope John when he flew into Andrews Air Force Base, and President Ford flew near our home in Lawton, Oklahoma. We missed shaking his hand by inches, but also got to see country singer Roy Clark who came to entertain for the President. I have been to lunches with Nancy Reagan, Mamie Eisenhower's granddaughter, Tipper Gore, Helen Thomas the news reporter, and Cokie Roberts, Katie Couric, as well as Colin Powell and his wife Alma, and author Alex Haley, Bob Hope, and President George W. Bush - really the list is too long. I was privileged to attend these luncheons with these people because of being an army wife and belonging to the Army Officers' Wives' Club of the Greater Washington Area. In addition, my husband was the on-call dentist to President Ford and had patients like Senators Strom Thurmond and Robert Dole. We even have a pewter platter in our china cabinet saying to my "good friend" William from Senator Strom Thurmond. I really would not call my husband his good friend, but it was nice to receive the platter.

The son of the Queen of Thailand was also a patient of my husband, so consequently when Queen Sirikit came to America we were invited not only to a dinner sponsored by the World Bank in her honor at the marvelous Hay Adams Hotel overlooking the White House in Washington, DC, on February

5, 1980, but we also had a private visit with the Queen in her hotel quarters. We were given instructions not to touch or shake the hands of the ladies in waiting and told how to greet the Queen. The hardest part for me as an Italian was the no touching part, and I nearly slipped up a couple of times. You don't realize how often you may touch someone until you are told not to do it. Cocktails were offered on the Pavilion and dinner in the President Adams room. The menu consisted of Bartard Montrachet 1977, Chataeu Lafite Rothschild 1970, Dom Perignon, Mousse De Foie Frais, Sauce Cumberland, Filet Mignon, Sauce Bearnaise, Puree do Carottes and Brocolis, Salade Adriatique, Sabayon, and Petits Fours Frais. Every morsel was delicious and the evening perfect for two young kids from Jersey.

Chapter Eleven

Times to Laugh

Children and their sayings have brought us humor throughout the years. My older daughter, then three years old, was having an upset stomach, and then the illness turned downward. She came running to me saying, "Oh, Mommy, my bottom vomited." Then the youngest daughter when she was two said to me one day, "I want the cat's soup." I said, "What do you mean?" She repeated it several times becoming more agitated by the minute, "I WANT the cat's soup." Finally, in desperation, I threw up my hands (typically Italian) and said, "Honey, I don't know what you want." We did have a cat named Mushroom and she finally said, "I want Mushroom soup." Ah, yes, good old Campbell's Cream of Mushroom Soup. One day my four-year-old son ran out the door and into the car. We were going for one of our Sunday drives. He did not know how to say any F's, so he remembered and said, "Oh, Mommy, You orgot to eed the ish." Well, we roared at this statement, to his chagrin, when we realized he was saying we forgot to feed the fish that we had in the tank. There is a commercial on television now with a very young baby looking at pictures of Presidents and naming each one by name. That was our oldest son when he was around two. He even astounded his own parents, not to mention friends and acquaintances, with words like hippopotamus and rhinoceros. We also get a kick out of other children's antics. My now bus driver husband had these wraparound sunglasses from having had cataract surgery. The first day of school two little boys got on the bus, and one stuck his neck out and slid his head from side to side and stared at my husband and said, "Can you see me?" The other child asked him, the driver, "Are you blind?" These school bus children voted Bill the best school bus driver they ever had and gave him a wonderful gift at Christmas time. It pays to see the humor in these small things because our life got really tough the first year I entered school, and our expenses skyrocketed with my tuition, so hence the job. In addition, one of my eighteen-year-old granddaughters came to live with us, and eventually she got a little kitty too. It had been close to over twenty years where the two of us lived alone in a nice quiet household, and things changed dramatically. Our children had all married and our own pets had died.

Chapter Twelve

Griswold Vacations

Once again in the story of my life I digress when I mention these years of just vacation fun and happenstance. Yet, these special times and incidences occupied a good portion of our lives, and the stories are the ones we repeat and enjoy over and over at family gatherings, so I feel I would be remiss not to document them in my memoir.

We enjoyed many more years of travel upon returning to the States, but with a name like Griswold (referring to the Griswold Vacation movies with actor Chevy Chase) we had our Griswold Vacation experiences as well. Sometimes now when we go out to eat and they put our name on a list and they call out "Griswold" I can hear some people giggle and say I wonder if that is Clark. So, now we say either Lu or Bill instead of Griswold. One day the UPS man asked my mother-in-law if her family tied her to the roof of the car. You would only understand that if you had seen those movies. Oddly, in Europe, no matter what country we visited, foreigners came up to me asking me directions. I must have the all country look or something. Why I spoke like this, I don't know, but in each country I would say when they asked directions, "I don't speak a de French, or I don't speak a de German." Had I gone out of my mind? My son visited us in Germany along with his family. When he got to the Information Desk he asked the man behind the counter very slowly, "Do   You   Speak   English?" The man leaned over the desk and stared at my son and said, "Yes   I   do!" When we were in Taiwan, the hotel clerk said to me, "You don't look American, you look pretty." I was afraid to ask her what on earth she thought Americans looked like if she thought I was pretty, so I just left it at that.

I nearly got arrested going from Egypt to Israel holding a stuffed camel when customs told me I could not bring the camel into Israel, and I should give it to the guard. I said no, explaining I was not going to leave it in Israel.

I was sending it home to my grandson in America. Two armed guards holding machine guns at that point came up to me, and I could see my husband's look of horror and chagrin. When it was obvious they were not going to back down I had to give up the toy camel, and I still resent this fact today.

On the last day of a cruise on the Western Caribbean I had gone shopping, and my husband had gone scuba diving. We had taken this cruise with friends. I came back to the ship around four o'clock and stopped at the pizza shop for a slice of pizza and then changed and went up on the deck to catch some rays. I thought I overheard the loud speaker saying my name, but I thought that was foolish, and they wouldn't do that on board ship. Then, I thought I heard it again, and I was thinking that if my friends were playing a joke on me they were really going to hear about it from me for sure as I was just beginning to relax. The third time though, I knew it was my name, and they were asking me to please go to the Concierge's Office. Then I started to get worried, and it got even worse when I stopped at the desk and the girl said, "Oh yes, let me get the Captain." He came out in his nice white crisp uniform, but looking rather grim. He said that my husband was in the hospital on the Grand Cayman Islands and I would need to evacuate the ship in thirty minutes because the ship was leaving port soon. He said he would send the girl down with me to help me clear my room. My friend and her husband also heard the message and came down to my room to help me pack all our stuff. I was throwing stuff here and there and we managed to get it all done except for a whole bag of shoes that would not fit in the cases. My friends offered to take the shoes back with them and each time when the story gets repeated the number of the shoes becomes larger and larger. They call me Imelda Marcos (a leader of the Philippine Government known for her excess number of shoes).

They put me in a large water taxi – just the girl helper from the cruise ship and me, and everyone on the ship looked over the railings as we drove away. They did provide a land taxi for me, and that is the last I ever heard from the cruise ship again. No one really knew what happened to my husband, and I did not know if he were dead or not.

The taxi driver asked me where I would like to go. I had not a clue. He told me the hotels on the beach where the American tourists stayed was a longer drive from the hospital, and there was a newer less extravagant hotel near the airport that was much closer to the hospital. I had to make a quick decision because the first thing I needed to do was to get rid of the excess luggage, then get to the hospital as fast as I could. I put all our essentials like passports and driver's licenses in one big beach bag that I carried around the whole time we were there. I made the decision to stay at the hotel closest to the hospital. We drove up in front of a new pink stucco structure. It was pleasant enough, but out in front stood a whole group of men all of a different race.

As a woman alone I stood out like a sore thumb in more ways than one. I felt intimated and frightened as they all watched and stared at this one woman with a ton of luggage. However, I also knew that had I been standing in front of a hotel and a taxi drove up with one person with a lot of luggage for two people, I would have stared too. I practically threw my stuff in the room and got my currency exchanged at the hotel desk. The staff was very accommodating and they called me another taxi, and off to the hospital I went. It was not bad enough that I was worried sick about my husband, but I was sitting in the taxi trying to figure the different currency and wondering how much tip to provide. Sometimes it just pays to be honest about your fears because the taxi driver told me of a cheaper fare taxi that I could hire for a day, and helped me to figure out the tip and everything.

The hospital was just a series of one-story hallways and not what one would expect a hospital to look like. They immediately brought me back to where my husband was being treated. At that point in time they had just been able to revive him from what would have been a death by drowning had he not survived. In his typical fashion he looked at me and made some type of funny remark to the amusement of the nurses and doctors. He was ordered to stay in the hospital a day or two for observation and then to remain on the island another couple of days. I went back to the hotel that evening and realized I was starved. It was nearly midnight, and I had only had a slice of pizza around four p.m. on the cruise ship. I ordered room service and they were so pleasant to me. Again, I was frightened to tell them I was alone, yet it was quite obvious. I had a feeling the proprietor who brought me my food knew, but I explained to him anyway and his genuine concern put me at ease. They treated me so well. I had not called anyone in my family up to this point. I thought it best to see at first the condition of my husband. I then got on the phone to call my children. Every one of them offered to come down and help to include my son-in-law, but I assured them at that point their Dad was all right and not to be concerned. My husband was released from the hospital after a few days and told to remain on the Island for a few more days of recovery. We spent the last few days touring the Grand Cayman Islands, the beaches, and relaxing by the hotel pool, and then we flew home later in the week. There is a spot on the Grand Cayman Islands called Hell, and it looks like what you might imagine Hell to be. We literally went to Hell and back. Fortunately, I had taken out specialty insurance that covered all our extra expenses. That was the best money I had ever spent.

My husband had been enjoying his scuba diving adventure when he began to feel fatigued. He noticed two of the people with him surface to the top, so he followed. They started swimming towards the boat that brought them out to the site, and Bill called to them, but they didn't hear him, and the next thing he passed out. Someone did discover him floating on the water, we know not who, and helped to save his life. Of course, the scuba diving company was extremely negligent not having someone with all the divers at all times. Our country gets maligned for its litigiousness, and perhaps rightly so. However, one has only to experience something like this to realize how at a loss you are though where a complaint means absolutely nothing. Several weeks after we returned home, a much younger man from our home area actually died on the same type of scuba diving expedition. He had very young children and the situation was very sad. I understand this is not as uncommon as we would like to think. We had a similar experience at one of the better hotels when in Yugoslavia where they had just watered some plants in huge ceramic pots. The pots leaked water that was invisible onto the tile floor, and my husband slipped and fell on his right hand. This was the very hand that he used to do most of his dental work. Fortunately he was not injured, but when we went to tell the hotel staff just so that no one else would be injured, they really could have cared less one way or the other, and they just shrugged their shoulders indifferently.

We had other strange experiences especially on cruises. I was walking the deck on one cruise in the middle of the ocean and got stung by a bee. As I passed the outdoor bar, I asked for some ice to rub on the area and continued my walk. Then we were leaving out of Philadelphia on a cruise to Bermuda. At the midnight buffet a young man told us one of our fellow passengers had died. Lord, I wondered, what did they do with the body? Was it refrigerated along with our food? I awoke the next morning to see the curtain at my porthole flying straight out over my head and not lying down flat against the window. I immediately realized what was happening when I became overcome with such seasickness. My husband who is frequently bothered by bouts of postural vertigo had taken pills to aid in this problem, but I didn't expect a problem, so I was not prepared. We encountered extremely rough seas, and the ship was rocking back and forth, and practically everyone on board became ill. This was a huge ship. They had barf bags deposited throughout all areas like containers for plants, and the stewards were handing them out as you would walk by. I guess there is a reason the Bermuda Triangle has a bad reputation. I have heard of many others on cruises to that area having the same type of experience. After things calmed down, I decided to enjoy the deck of the ship when I heard this horrible loud motorized whirring sound and looked up. Hovering over the ship was a medical-evacuation helicopter. They lowered a basket and put a woman inside who had broken her hips and transported her away. I will say one thing; our vacations have not been dull. I must add that a sixteen-day cruise that brought us through the Panama Canal was wonderful.

Chapter Twelve

Once, when visiting the big Island of Hawaii we took the walking tour over the live volcano. The smell of sulfur was stifling, and as we walked over the charred area a fog and mist appeared. The guide would walk ahead to spot the white markings on the rocks of volcanic ash, and when she left us we could not even see her the fog got so bad. The sulfur smell even got worse. I thought, "Oh, my God, she will never return. Our whole family is going to die out here in this desolation." Somehow that guide got us back safely, but many weeks later in the local paper they had been interviewing the guides, and the one exclaimed about the day she could not see the markings because of the fog and how frightened even she was, so I knew my own fear was not unfounded.

We often took a few of our grandchildren at a time to our condo at the beach. They would bring their motorized scooters and we would go boating on the Rocket Ship.

In the evening, after walking the boardwalk, we sometimes rented videos for them. One year they wanted to rent the same video over and over again. The video was about someone called Jimmy Neutron, and some children in the story escaped from home and they kept repeating, "My clothes don't match, my clothes don't match. I'm out in public and my clothes don't match." This became our mantra. The children sang it over and over and over, and it got stuck in my mind until I kept hearing it over and over and over. It nearly drove me crazy! Ah, the joys of being a grandparent.

I babysat for at least four of my grandchildren on a daily basis when they were younger when their parents took jobs outside the home at different times and ages. I felt a certain gratitude at being able to help those that needed it. Often we flew to our other children's homes to baby sit while those parents could have well earned time alone with each other, or to help if one of the children were hospitalized, and of course to take care of the siblings when a new sister or brother came along. One time a granddaughter was born in Florida around spring break time, and I boarded a plane filled with spring-breakers. Actually, I had a ball on that flight. The students sure had fun teasing me.

I recently finished reading a book called *Tough Choices: A Memoir* written by Carly Fiorina who was the famous prior CEO of Hewlett Packard. Fortune Magazine voted her the most powerful woman in business. She had opportunities in her life that were not available when I was younger, yet in retrospect I was very content with my life the way it was. I enjoyed traveling as I did, and I treasured the fact that I could stay home with my children when they were young because once they are grown you can never go back. I appreciated the time I had to take these vacations after many years of not being able to afford them while we worked to advance our lives. According to Ms. Fiorina, she had to sacrifice freedom and spontaneity to achieve her status in life. I did not have to sacrifice any of that, and for this I am grateful.

Chapter Thirteen

Learning to Endure

There really are no words that can explain the feelings I endured when my mother died. To look at her the month before she died one would have thought her the picture of health. Even our local pharmacist was shocked when he heard the news of her death. I remember a very pretty lady whose pictures don't do her justice at all. There was this rosy glow that emanated from her. One day walking through town with her while I was in high school we passed my English teacher who acknowledged us. Later the next day in school he asked me who the beautiful woman was that was with me, and I explained to him it was my mother. That this esteemed gentleman should remark this way about my mother filled me with such pride. I also used to have young children who had met my mother come up to me and tell me how nice they thought she was.

Sometimes she would get angry at something I would do, and when she did the tone of her voice let me know immediately that I had better straighten up or else. My mother did not mind throwing around a swear word once in a while, but there was no way she was going to let those words come out of my mouth. One day, I became angry at something and spouted out "Oh, nuts!" You would have thought I used the foulest language there was when she yelled back at me, "Don't you ever let me hear you saying that again." To this day you still won't hear a swear word come out of my mouth.

I had been married several years, and we were living in Maryland with our sixteen-month-old son. My husband was in the middle of studying for his mid-semester final exams. This was right after New Year's Eve. Later I had seen a picture of the family with my mother taken that New Year's Eve. She looked just fine. We got a phone call saying that my mother was ill and in the hospital, so my husband made plans to take me up to Jersey. He then returned to school in preparation for his exams. We only had the one car. Those were very hard days. My son did not really know a lot of the aunts and grandmothers and great grandmothers who watched him while I would spend my days at the hospital. His schedule became all out of sorts, and he would cry half the night. My husband had always been so good about taking turns with me when the baby was like that, but here I was alone. I lay in bed holding him and crying right along with him. I was so sad and so fatigued. One night my aunt (the beauty who never married) heard me and walked in the room so gentle and sweet saying, "Oh you poor sweetheart, how hard this must be for you." As hard as it was however, no one expected my mother was going to die. She was only forty-four years old after all.

One day I went into her room of the hospital only to find it emptied out of everything and the bed made. What a fright that was. I later found out they had just transferred her to another unit (probably intensive care). Exactly thirty-one days after she was brought to the hospital just for observation she had died. I was sitting in the room with her when it appeared she was having difficulty breathing. There was this odd noise coming out of her mouth. I later learned they called this the death rattle. I called the nurses to come in, and they sent me out of the room. Certainly, had I known or expected she was dying; I would have stayed there to comfort her and tell her I loved her. People were not always so verbally expressive of their love in those days. All the adults certainly were very loving to my children, and me, as they would give us affectionate pinches on our cheeks and say, "Como si bella." At least that is what I heard and felt it was something good. We got hugged and kissed a lot and those were returned by us with pleasure. But this day–nothing–just the nurses coming out to tell me my mother had died. No one ever let me know how seriously ill she was. Perhaps they didn't know it themselves. The death certificate said chronic kidney disease, arteriosclerosis, and hardening of the arteries. The whole situation was so very sad really, but it didn't really hit me until after the funeral.

One thing I didn't like at the funeral was the people standing and sitting around talking and laughing when I felt so sad. Having now experienced death a multitude of times, I know how important this interaction was, but then it did not seem right. My aunts had asked me what I would like to do with my mother's wedding rings. I said to bury them with her. I felt it did not seem right to remove her wedding rings from her. We were all so devastated later that no one said to me that perhaps I should keep the rings as I might have a daughter someday that might enjoy having them as a memento of their grandmother. Of course, I eventually did have two daughters. Since I was an only child my relatives could only give me advice, but all the decisions were left to me, and in retrospect that might not have been a good decision, but at that time I could not see removing the rings from my mother's fingers.

When we got back to the house the whole family sat around the dining room table for a meal like we had done so many times before. I looked around the table at everyone and suddenly it hit me that my mother was not there. Furthermore, she would never be there again. This horrible wave of emotion came over me. I ran upstairs and threw myself on the bed in such despair. My husband and some aunts tried to console me, but I knew things would never be the same. Later, there were about six years in a row that someone very close to me died. Life goes on and you never forget, but you adjust.

My mother used to take me on big shopping trips to the city twice a year or more for holiday clothes and back to school clothes. Though she was a single Mom I never wanted for anything, and we would get back home and they would have me model the clothes and shoes and it was fun to hear the "oohs" and "aahs." After her job in the Defense Plant she went to work as a waitress in a very fancy restaurant called the Button Wood Manor that is on a lake in our hometown and is still in business today. We had our fiftieth high school reunion there. She received wonderful tips, and I was never at a loss for money. She eventually became the head hostess and befriended a wealthy couple that dined at the restaurant frequently. When they found out she had a daughter, they wanted to meet me. Plans were made for them to pick me up one night when my mother was at work. This huge black limousine drove up in front of our home just to come for me. I felt like such a little princess driving away in this chauffeured driven car to a delightful dinner with some very endearing people.

One thing I did not enjoy was when my mother or my aunts would ask me to play the piano for guests. I would do it because I didn't know how to graciously get out of it. I studied classical music (though you would never know it today) and could play the Minute Waltz in a minute, though I much preferred "boogie-woogie." I still like peppy songs and in another life I would have much rather been a dancer than work in an office. My Mom did take me once for an audition in New York City, but later decided that was not what she wanted for me. My cousin studied piano at the Julliard School of Music, but when we would get together we would play chopsticks and sing popular tunes to our piano playing. One of my best friends and I always used to harmonize, and we were asked to sing duets at her Methodist Church. I did play a piano solo at my eighth grade graduation. The song was "The Anvil Chorus." I once even played for money for a group of businessmen, but I was really out of my element there. Today, I love to hear even rap music. I really enjoy all music, and I will dance at the drop of a feather. While walking is my favorite exercise, when the weather is nasty outside I will put on some peppy music and dance around the house, still today, at my age. My husband comes in and looks at me, and I am sure he is wondering to himself, "What have I got myself here?" We do enjoy walking together for exercise and can get into some hot conversations on our walks. One day we spent thirty minutes walking and arguing about who was the smartest between MDs, PhDs and other doctorates. Don't even ask how that got started.

My mother, Ruth Mazzei Sciarappa, was a gracious friendly woman, and I hope I have learned these special traits from her. She loved to sing like I do, and she was happy most of the time though her temper fuse could be a little short. Fortunately, her anger was rarely, if ever, directed at me. She especially adored her first grandchild (my first born son), and I know she would have been so thrilled to meet my other three children and her twelve great grandchildren that followed. Ruth was always working, so I would be home during the day with my grandparents. However, Ruth made all the important decisions in my life like if I could go to the beach during vacation week or go to a function with a boy. When she was at home, my Mom would plan a day of fun with me. We would go shopping, or visiting with friends which people liked to do when I was young. She was forward thinking and ahead of her time where women are concerned, and I believe I received a lot of my gumption from her. Ruth was not an old fashioned Italian American woman at all.

Chapter Fourteen

Simple Times

Sometimes when I look back life seemed so simple. Whether it was, or not, I can't say for sure. While my present life is definitely a good life, undoubtedly the simple life was good too. We did not have big supermarkets, but would go to the local A&P store and stand behind a counter and tell our order to a sales clerk. We would say, "One box of cereal, that one up there." We would point and the clerk would use a grabber for things up high. This was not so pleasant a task though when we had to go to the pharmacy and ask the man behind the counter for feminine products. On the opposite side of the A&P store from the groceries was the butcher. I never learned the cuts of meat so I would be petrified shortly after I got married not knowing what to order. I sure was happy when the supermarkets became established, and I could just walk along and pick out any meat that looked good to me.

In a houseful of women I never really learned how to cook. All those wonderful Italian recipes and I only got one from my grandmother, and it is for cheese balls. They look like meatballs, but they have no meat. I cannot even be sure they are traditional Italian fare as no other Italian friends with whom I speak ever heard of them. My grandmother did most of the cooking since most of us women in the household were either working or in school. When the rest of us did cook it was to make fun things like cakes, puddings and desserts, and non-Italian food. I did help to clean after dinner and one time–and don't ask me why-I decided to carry about eight plates in a pile to the cabinets. I slipped and they all fell, breaking every one. I felt terrible, but no one yelled at me. They were concerned I was not hurt. Again, this was not a supposedly typical Italian reaction that one sees portrayed in the movies and on television. As I got older I acquired some of the other Italian recipes we all enjoy.

When desiring to write one's memoirs it helps to read the stories of others who have done the same. I especially chose to read some books by other Italian Americans. I began to see in spite of my total Italian heritage, I was somehow different, and I wanted to know why. The first book I read was called *Crazy in the Kitchen: Food, Feuds, and Forgiveness in an Italian American Family*. This was a marvelous book by Louise DeSalvo. I thought we had so much in common at first as she was raised in New Jersey, like I was, and had a grandmother that was a big influence in her life, like I had. Her life situation could not have been more different from mine however. While the author was not allowed to cook, and she had the desire, I am sure if I had the desire someone would have taken the time to teach me. The women in her home had some tough issues in their lives that affected their personalities that trickled down to the author. If the women in my home had tough issues, I was never made aware of them. Our home always had an abundance of food. We had many different men delivering items to our home like a milkman, an iceman who brought huge blocks of ice (until refrigerators became common), a man that delivered eggs, and one delivering olive oil in huge cans. I was use to hearing the egg man yell out, "Egg Man." So, when I moved to Baltimore I could hear someone in my back yard one time saying what I thought was "Egg Man." I went over to the window and said, "No, thank you." The man yelled back "I am the meter man lady, here to read your gas meter." I felt like such a jerk.

I especially enjoyed going over to my grandmother's sister's home. It had a lovely big staircase similar to the staircase in the movie *Gone with the Wind*, though not as large. When we visited, she used to just call the grocer down the street, and he would bring over the food she requested. I could hear her tell him to just put it on the bill. In Herbert J. Gans's book *The Urban Villagers* about Italian-Americans living in the West End of Boston, those shopkeepers also let the villagers put their purchases on a bill, but normally people paid cash for everything. I thought this sounded so exciting, to just say, "Put it on my bill." My favorite thing to eat at her house was the packaged bread that came already sliced and topped with peanut butter and jelly. Now, what kind of Italian is that? This great-aunt had a son and daughter that were like a brother and sister to me. We would go on trips together and fight like siblings too. Her son was the best man in our wedding.

Today we put wreaths on our doors for decorative purposes. When I was a child and you saw a wreath on a door it meant that someone in that family had just died. In one way it did seem like a good way to let others in the neighborhood know of the family death. They also had quarantine signs put on doors of those children who got the measles or other contagious diseases, and this happened to me. No one outside the family was allowed to come into the home during these quarantines. Being sick was not always a bad thing. The children from my class would draw pictures and write notes and leave them at the door for my Mom to give to me. I would be treated to jello, ice cream and all kinds of good things. The doctor always came to the home instead of us having to go to him when we were really sick. We only went to the doctor's office for check-ups or minor ailments. This custom was stopped by the time I was an adult, but the town doctor always continued to come to our home to care for my grandparents when they became quite elderly, and for that we were always most thankful.

My relatives seemed to follow one custom of the second generation of Italians that I read about in *Crazy in the Kitchen* and *The Urban Villagers* in that this second generation was not that interested in identifying with Italy. I do not believe my relatives were intentionally avoiding this identification. The second generation was reacting to the only thing they were used to. Realistically, in my opinion, they were in America to stay, so why not acclimate to the ways of the new country? I did not live in Germany for three years and expect them to conform to my American ways. I adjusted and enjoyed their customs and lifestyle, and this is what I believe this second generation was doing. I feel it was only later that they realized once their parents died they would lose all memories of the family's Italian history, and it eventually became the trend to embrace one's heritage. This proved to be especially true during the 1960's and 1970's when the television show *Roots* became a national phenomenon along with celebrating the nation's Bicentennial. Of course there were many who purposely avoided their Italian American heritage because of abuse they suffered and prejudice against them. Many were pre-determined to be blacks because of their darker skin color and darker hair. They were just disliked because of their ethnicity and because they were Italians. One way of purposely avoiding their ethnicity was to change or replace the vowel on their last name to make it appear non-Italian. I can appreciate their reasons for wanting this change, but others who did not suffer were just getting on with life in a new country.

I know outside our home the women acted like white Anglo Saxon Protestants, though they were brought up Catholic and Italian. This was not an affectation and they were not at all ashamed of their heritage. They worked for lawyers and accountants doing executive work, and keeping of the books, and it was just how they became acclimated. At home, they spoke to their parents in Italian and enjoyed the Italian customs. Not one of my aunts married Italians either, so that probably had a lot to do with their actions. Two married Polish men, and two married WASPS (white Anglo-Saxon Protestants).

While the women in *Crazy in the Kitchen* were constantly fighting, the few times I can ever remember a good fight I knew something pretty bad had happened (like when one of my young aunts eloped). They yelled about it, and the next day it was forgotten.

My grandparents also spoke fondly of their old country. Apparently my relatives came from all over Italy because though my father and mother both have dark hair and eyes, as I do, many of the relatives, especially on my father's side, were blonde and blue-eyed. Author DeSalvo did marvelous research on her Italian background, and I could learn from some of her research that I might probably assume that my relatives perhaps came to this country because of harsh working conditions though I never got this impression. One would imagine that if things were up to par in their own country they might never have left in the first place. My grandmother was only sixteen years old when she did come to America, so in her case I would suppose she was just following her parents. My great-grandparents were already married when they arrived in the United States, so theirs was not an arranged marriage either. Most likely they came here to leave volatile, incorrigible and oppressive situations caused by war and other factors. Social scientists talk about the "push" and "pull" factors on why people migrate. Sometimes it is about leaving something bad, but sometimes it is looking for something good too. My family probably had as much "push" as they did "pull" since they already seemed fairly secure and well set. Perhaps they had a dream of finding greater opportunities in America than what they had in Italy. My relatives also were publicly educated and had skills like shoemakers and barbers, so there was no need to escape harsh working conditions in the fields as those relatives in *Crazy in the Kitchen* and *The Urban Villagers*. With the exception of the delightful story *Rosa: The Life of an Italian Immigrant* by Marie Hall Ets, the majority of the books I read were about Italians who immigrated from southern Italy. Most of them came to America, according to the stories, because of harsh, poverty stricken living conditions. Because so many of the southern Italians had their stories documented, there was this tendency to lump all immigrants together, but this was not obviously the case with my grandparents nor with the above mentioned Rosa who came from northern Italy in the silk-making village of Lombardy. Like the women in my family, Rosa was not subservient. She was feisty and determined, and when things worked against her she was smart enough to scrutinize the situation and take charge to see that it was rectified. Fortunately, a young social worker that became acquainted with Rosa was astute enough to document what is probably one of the few immigrant stories told about a woman.

Chapter Fifteen

Establishing a Lifestyle

I can still remember one of the nicest compliments that I had ever received. Everyone gets the usual nice compliments about appearance, looks or intelligence, but this one meant more to me than any of those surface compliments i.e. with the exception of my intelligence. I was leaving my job at Sears to go to Germany, and the other workers were throwing me a going away party. One lovely woman came up to me (the wife of an IBM executive) and said, "We are really going to miss you as you are the one person that gave this place some class." What better compliment can one give not only to me, but to the Italian American people in general? So often authors achieve fame by writing only about the derogatory aspects of their lives, but what does this conjure up in the minds of people not familiar with your kind?

I often wonder who in society decided that our immigrants were lower class members of our society. Italian Americans were expected to assimilate as white ethnics. Were the people who decided this from Northern Europe and the colder climates? They after all are going to be startlingly white because of their long cold winters and lack of daylight and sunshine. Many did rationalize why whites were supposedly superior to other "races." Did it not occur to some that those Italians who were dark came from southern Italy where it was sunny and warm and of course they would be tanned? People from places closer to the equator are darker because over the millennia their skin has adapted in color to let them withstand the sun's stronger rays. Some Italians from the lower boot part of the country may have intermarried with the Africans whose country was in close proximity. In the long run they all emigrated here from different countries in Europe, so no one really had the right to tell another who should assimilate and who should not. Someday I predict we are all going to be beige anyway.

After reading about other Italian Americans and their customs, I began to realize why I was different. A lot had to do with my family's lifestyle and the area where I lived. The stereotypical Italian American experience is much more of an urban one and where I lived, while not exactly rural, was definitely not urban living. Most of my neighbors were not Italian either. In my younger years, as well as today, I had friends that were very wealthy and some that were quite the other extreme. Some of my friends lived on farms. I was exposed to milking cows and seeing pigs, and we got to ride our friends' horses. All these places were within short and long walking distances though from my home. Many of my friends had live rabbits for pets. At Easter time I remember receiving little colored baby chicks. I think this custom of artificially dyeing chicks has now been outlawed. Some of the homes were so fancy we were not allowed to sit on the couches in the living room. One family on our street was quite poor in comparison to the others in the same neighborhood. I was delighted when they offered me bread that was spread with butter and sugar. I guess you can see I always had a sweet tooth. One day when I was playing at this home I used the bathroom. As I was leaving the room, the mother said to me, "Why don't you go to the bathroom in your own house?" Nice lady.

The layout of our town consisted mainly of three streets running parallel to one another. Main Street was the longest and was the place that held the businesses, movie house, soda shops, pharmacy, library and post office. Most of the physicians also had their practices in homes on Main Street. The upper end had fancy homes, and the lower end that was several miles away ended near the lake and the railroad tracks where we could get the train to New York City. Broad Street was where I lived, and most of this street just had single-family homes or duplexes. Many of the homes had front porches where people would sit and speak to the passersby. Homes of the wealthy people would be alongside those of the middle class and the occasional home of the poor as they were all mingled together. The grammar and high schools were also at the upper end of Broad Street and about two blocks from my home, and many of the teachers lived in the surrounding homes. On a few of the side streets were the lakes where we would swim. The third parallel street, Church Street, was much shorter and there were a few businesses there, but mostly homes of blacks and a few whites. While the blacks were essentially separated in where they lived, we knew most of the black families, and they knew most of the white families. Children from all the homes, no matter their color or race, went to the same schools, and if there was any prejudice at all I was not aware of it. Yet, as I think back, I realize that while we coexisted peacefully there was still a very real sense of social separation. Neither the blacks nor the whites invited each other to play in their homes except for sporting event parties where all members of the teams were included regardless of race. We also all played together at least when we were at school on the playground. Two houses from ours a family had a barn in the backyard, and we loved jumping from the second floor of the barn unto mattresses set on the ground. How we did not break bones I'll never understand. Most of the homes had lovely yards where we had cookouts, played croquet, or hide and seek and kick-the-can. We sometimes had pet contests and gave plays for the adults or each other. On certain holidays we could sit on our porch and watch the parade go by. If we bought ice cream cones in town and walked home eating them in the hot summer, we had to eat really fast because the ice cream would melt down our arms. By the time we got home we were all sticky. There were only a few Italians in our entire neighborhood among a mixture of ethnicities. While we obviously all had a different social class structure, it did not affect our living and socializing together. It was not until I started to write this memoir that I began to see that the way I lived probably had a lot to do with the type of Italian I am today. I already explained I did not live in the stereotypical Italian American urban neighborhood. Yet, my neighborhood was not completely rural either. While I could walk to the farms, we lived closer to the center of town, so it was more a small town atmosphere. I became more fully aware that my background was as much atypical Italian as typical. It also became apparent that ethnic identity is by no means a standardized thing within any given group. I will discuss this more in a later chapter.

I had some unusual pets. One pet was a very small sized turtle, in addition to the colored chickens and a dog named Spot. For some reason, I also had a black crow. I can't remember his name, but knowing my originality with the dog named Spot, the crow was probably named Blackie. The crow was kept in a back shed that we got to by walking under a grape arbor (reminiscent of Italy). My friends were all fascinated by this unusual pet, and things were going well until one day the crow got into the leftover house paint we kept in the sheds. Unfortunately, that was the end of that crow.

My aunts also had some extremely wealthy friends and many times we got to visit some huge estates. We stayed several nights in one that had nine bathrooms with marble everywhere and an enormous kitchen. It was so huge my mother was rather apprehensive staying there especially considering the location was deep down a long driveway and situated in a woods. The estate was near Gettysburg, Pennsylvania, and the radio station was WSBA. My young aunt used to get such a kick out of the announcer who used to say, "This is station W ass B A."

Holidays were always the best. My aunts did a marvelous job of decorating. They used to put silver tinsel on the trees and hung each one individually, and the silver would sparkle along with the much larger colored tree lights that were in use at that time. Because of the dry heat in the homes the tree would not be put up until Christmas Eve, and it would come down New Year's Day when you could hear the needles falling off the tree onto the floor. We had a huge metal grate between the living room and dining room (before the heat was converted to more modern means) that blew heat up from the furnace. I enjoyed standing over it in my dress and having the heat blow up the dress on a very cold day, but the dry heat was hard on fresh trees. People use to come around caroling, and we would always give them refreshments. One time my Presbyterian minister came by with a group of singers to sing to me (Christmas caroling) because I was ill, and he gave me a big fat whopper of a kiss right on the mouth. What that was all about I still don't know. I was a Presbyterian at the time and I can remember the Sunday school teachers reading *Mrs. Wiggly and the Cabbage Patch* for the children instead of some Biblical study. This minister did offer me a scholarship to a religious school in Tennessee, but my aunt and uncle who lived in Alfred, New York wanted me to go to school near them. I did go to school at Alfred University in New York State at the age of seventeen, but my aunt and uncle moved to Caracas, Venezuela with his job (an offer so good he could not refuse), so perhaps that was not one of my better choices. I had to take a thirteen-hour train trip to get to the school and it was really tough trying to take everything I would need for several months on the train. The distance involved in getting to Alfred and the fact that my relatives were no longer there meant that my expenses were greater staying in a dormitory. These were but some of the reasons why I did not return to college my sophomore year.

I was baptized a Catholic when I was a baby, but we were unable to get to the Catholic Church very often because we would have had to go to the next town, and the only car in our home belonged to my aunt. Our own town did not have a Catholic Church. When my aunt would go to church I would go with her. Otherwise, I became quite active in the churches of my friends and as a teen joined the Presbyterian Church. When my husband and I started planning for our wedding and wanted to make arrangements for the church, he wanted first to tell his parents since he was Catholic. His intentions were to get married in my church and change his religion for me. When he later came to my home, and I asked him how his conversation went with his parents, he said his mother started crying. This really upset me because I was very fond of my future mother-in-law, and I didn't like getting off on the wrong track so to speak. After much consideration, I decided to re-evaluate becoming Catholic again. There are big differences in the two churches concerning communion and some other factors, but I decided I could live with the changes. I have been devout in the Catholic religion from the first day we got married. While I sometimes become irritated at some happenings in the way our church handles certain things, I voice my opinion when I feel it is necessary, and I work things out in my own mind for me personally. I have never been sorry about my decision.

Throughout the years there were always loads of toys and clothes under the tree, and the best toy was when Santa brought me my big red two-wheel bike. Friends always came over and we would share showing our gifts. I loved when the adults' friends came over because of the wonderful licorice smell of the anisette drink they would serve.

Of all the toys I can remember though that made a big impression on me was not actually something I received, but it was a gift given to my cousin who went to Julliard. She had a box of five little baby dolls all tucked together in a row depicting the Dionne Quintuplets, with five little bottles, and five little outfits. Something about those babies used to fascinate me even as I got older, and they were relegated to my cousin's attic. I would ask if we could go up there to see them. I sure wish I knew where those dolls were today. Multiple births were most unusual in those days without in vitro fertilization. The five little Dionne babies were identical quintuplets born in Canada in 1934, and the odds of this type of birth were one in fifty-seven million at that time, so these children were indeed a novelty. Unfortunately, according to the stories at the time, they were taken from their parents during their younger years and exploited by the Canadian government.

I tried carrying on the tradition of not decorating our tree until Christmas Eve. Unfortunately, we so over-indulged our first baby with toys that when he came from his room on Christmas morning and saw so many things, the tree was almost an afterthought. Then one Christmas Eve my husband, who was forever a student and forever working someplace, came home from his job. We were not used to drinking because we couldn't afford liquor or beer for one thing, and our time was better spent. However, at his job they kept offering him drinks because of the holiday, and he, not used to drinking, came home a little tipsy. That Christmas Eve when he climbed up on the ladder to hang a decoration high on the tree, he fell off the ladder and into the tree. From that day on I decided to put the tree up weeks before to enjoy before "Santa" came.

Picking trees used to cause some of our biggest fights too. My husband would go to the lot and like the first one he saw. I wanted to examine the whole lot and pick the perfect tree, but the tree was never perfect. In other more practical issues in my life I was by no means a perfectionist, but I was certainly obsessed with having the perfect tree. Perhaps I wanted my tree to look as good as the ones when I was younger, and my aunts hung each piece of tinsel individually. What I didn't realize was that they had all kinds of help and no little baby to watch. We always had to move the tree around to the best side and hide the ugly side. Some years we had to tie the tree to the wall to keep it from falling. In Oklahoma, I hung real cookies shaped like Santa and Christmas Trees etc., on the tree only to wake up the next morning to see that the tree toppled over and the dog had eaten all the cookies. Another time in Hawaii I thought I found the most perfect tree, and we picked it out pretty fast only to have the sales person squeeze it into a plastic bag and break off the top. I was so disappointed I wanted to scream, so I went out and bought a fake tree perfect in shape, and for many years we had two trees, one fake and one real. When we purchased the stand for the fake tree we didn't know it revolved, meaning I had to decorate every inch of the tree. We could push a button, and it would play the song "Silent Night." Yes, I know, that was corny.

We also tried taking hayrides out into the woods and cutting down real trees. One time in New Mexico we got off track and started running like crazy when we saw bear prints in the snow. I always hung real candy canes on my trees, and I continued to do so in Hawaii. My neighbor told me that was not a good idea because they would melt. I thought she must be crazy as I felt this hard piece of candy in my hand, and I didn't listen but hung them on the tree. Well, you guessed it. I went out that day, and when I returned I had melted globs of "goo" all over the place. If it were Oklahoma I could better understand with the 115-degree heat, but Hawaii and eighty-five degrees all year long? I guess it was the humidity as well, something we did not get much of in Oklahoma. We had to keep our lights on in our closets in Hawaii so our shoes would not mildew.

As the previous anecdotes suggest, life is full of little rituals, habits and traditions that we carry down from our families throughout the years. These traditions help us to bring consistency to our lives, while establishing our own lifestyle. In some incomprehensible way reviving these traditions in our home, when we lived far away from family, helped us to feel closer to the relatives we left behind. Our children also carry on many of the traditions that my husband and I reinvented and created.

Chapter Sixteen

Feeling Italian

What is it like to feel Italian? Would it be the way we dress? How about the food we eat? The way we speak, or our mannerisms? If I had to make a guess I would say my husband feels more Italian than I do—and his heritage is anything but Italian. He absolutely loves Italian food and used to say he wanted to date me so he could open my grandmother's refrigerator to retrieve the huge rolls of salami, among other things. He went to a Catholic grammar school that had a lot of Italian students attending, and at lunch time every day he looked forward to switching sandwiches with them—a sausage and pepper sandwich for regular old lunch meat.

It certainly could not be the way we look, because some of us are dark and others are light skinned. Kym Ragusa in her book *The Skin Between Us: A Memoir of Race, Beauty, and Belonging* complained about her curly hair. I would give a million bucks to have some curl in my hair which is soft, fine, silky, and extremely straight. For years I have spent countless hours getting home permanents, or setting my hair in bobby pins or hot rollers to help it curl. At my eighth grade graduation I went in to the neighboring town of Keyport to a friend's beauty salon and had my hair done in a lovely pageboy (where the ends are all curled under). Then I rode home on the bus on that warm June day and opened the bus window for some fresh air and "poof" the pageboy was gone as well as the money we spent to get it done.

Thomas J. Ferraro, author of *Feeling Italian: The Art of Ethnicity in America* asserts, "Italians learned the love of feeling Italian not necessarily from Italy but from the artwork of artists like Guiseppe Michele Stella (later to be known as Joseph Stella), that brought out the steel and intensity of New York City through his paintings, wanting to both claim and declaim in visual form the "steely" orchestra of modern constructions." (Ferraro 2005). We absorb some of our customs, according to Ferraro, through "mutual mythmaking of the most intimate order. One hundred years of cultural reciprocity is a simple idea, really: as the Italians have gotten more American, so the Americans have gotten more Italian." (Ferraro 2005). We perhaps get our inner Italian feelings from the many famous artists like Frank Sinatra, Bruce Springsteen and Madonna who all were of Italian descent. However, I felt Ferraro gave these performers too much credence. I appreciated their talent, but never put them on a pedestal or idolized any of them. As for *The Godfather* motion picture series and The *Sopranos* that I have only seen once or twice, they too are only pieces of imaginary tales to be enjoyed. To me they are entertainment and just that. These stories are fiction with just a tinge of the truth, depicting only the fringe members of the Italian American race. I did not take pleasure of their life style as Ferraro stated, and I never had a desire to live or act the way the Corleones did. Does this make me any less of an Italian? I am not trying in any way or manner to deny the influence these Italian entertainers and other media forms of entertainment have on our society. They are a prevalent and important part of our popular culture, just like the famous artists were from our past. I am entertained when I see the shows or hear the music just like everyone else, and I do admire the fame they have achieved. I just don't idolize their talents. I would be much more inclined to idolize someone in my own family.

Another author Edvige Giunta, who wrote *Writing with an Accent: Contemporary Italian American Women Authors,* attempted to give us a feeling of being Italian when she featured the work of some brilliant Italian American women authors from the late 1970's to the early 1980's. Metaphorically, we learn how these vibrant women authors document the Italian American culture through their own personal writing accent. They take into account many issues like societal and familial abuse as well as many other factors in their documentation. I found the fact that the three female Italian American authors whose books I chose to read (DeSalvo, Ragusa and Giunta) all knew each other and I could not help but think how great that would be to get to know each and every one. All three authors' writings helped me realize how the way I was brought up was very different than a lot of Italians mostly because of the small town in which I lived. I did not live in a city full of other Italians as my neighbors.

One day in 1992, when we were living in Maryland, I got a generic letter from Lee Iococca asking if I would like to honor any relatives who came to America through Ellis Island. My grandmother was nearing 100 years old at the time (she lived to be 102), and I thought this would make a wonderful permanent gift of her life. Our family gave my grandmother a huge 100th birthday party where she was serenaded by all the men in the family including my husband, sons and cousins. They wore straw hats and canes and sang "*Oh you Beautiful Doll*." She was also known to get up behind a microphone and belt out a tune at a wedding. The Mayor of our town issued a proclamation for my Grandmother to have her own special day where she was honored. If you go to Ellis Island you will see her name on a wall there as Philomena (Filomena) Mazzei. It was not but a few months later I got another letter from Iococca saying that as a relative of someone who came through Ellis Island I was eligible to also have my name inscribed on the wall. They obviously needed money, so I thought why not? I decided to have my name written with my maiden name inserted since Griswold is rather a common name, and while Lucille is not common it could still be conceivable that there might be another Lucille Griswold, but I was pretty sure there would not be another Lucille Sciarappa Griswold. One day I went with some members of my family on the ferry to Ellis Island, and it was indeed a thrill to see both our names there. In the background of a picture of us taken on the ferry are the Twin Towers still standing proud before September 11, 2001. Now, that feels Italian having my name alongside all the other immigrants from all over Europe who came to the United States with such marvelous dreams.

Unfortunately, for some, those dreams did not always materialize as was noted in Stefano Luconi's book *From Paesani to White Ethnics: The Italian Experience in Philadelphia*. We learn how poverty-stricken they were when arriving and how they were treated as a dark race, shunned and discriminated against. They all would congregate and live in an area like Philadelphia, staying among their own ethnic group, and attending Catholic churches just for Italians. Religion was more embedded in their lives having a church within walking distance and having mostly people of the same ethnicity going to the same church. My life as an Italian American was nothing like this. The lives of my Italian American friends were lives pretty much like my own in a small, non-segregated town though most did not live near me. Most of them also lived in lovely single family homes. This was one of the biggest differences I noticed about my own heritage, knowing I did not live in a closed community of only other Italians, but had neighbors of many races and religions. Yet, similar customs permeated the inside of our homes like when my grandparents dropped oil into water in a bowl and depending on what the oil did the relatives would be happy or sigh sadly. This was called *il malocchio* or evil eye. The author Kym Ragusa also talked about this experience. To me the oil always looked like it did the same thing in the water, and I never really understood the whole procedure, except they usually did this in our home when someone was feeling ill, or so it seemed to me.

I was aware of how the Italians had derogatory names shouted at them, like dagos, guineas and wops (a term derived from the phrase "without papers"), though no one ever said them to me. I also heard other races being maligned with words like kike, limey and kraut, and I will not even go into the most objectionable "n" word. It was not just the Italians that suffered these names. Things change as well. Today the words Negro and oriental are considered offensive, and they were not offensive in my day. I have an old dictionary to back me on this statement. The preferred words today would be black and Asian. I just think it was a reflection of the times or a period of personal insecurity where people had to disparage one another for some strange feeling of self-importance. We were always taught the little ditty, "Sticks and stones can break my bones, but names can never hurt me." Of course we all know that names hurt a lot, and I was happy to see for the most part people stopped resorting to this nonsense as I grew older. Unfortunately though, lately this appears to be reappearing. My own family did experience some name calling when we moved to Hawaii and we were called "haoles." It was the white person there that was being disparaged. The word definitely had a negative connotation when said to white people, but I learned early on to just tell my children not to be offended by it as it mostly meant we were white and different. My children went to the public schools with the native Hawaiians, and we managed just fine and actually loved living there for four years.

Because I married young and changed my name to my husband's last name which was the custom at that time, most new people did not know my ethnicity. Only after associating with these new acquaintances when I moved away from home did I begin to sense that some people had a prejudice against Italians. This was easy to tell by the jokes they told, or belittling statements they made in front of me not knowing they were disparaging me. I would stop them by saying, "Before you go any further I suggest you stop what you are saying right now or you might embarrass yourself." Other times I might just leave the group if I didn't feel they were worth knowing in the first place. I also had some same experiences that were in common with my ancestors when I went to live in Germany for three years. I was thrown into a totally different culture and language, and contrary to popular belief not all foreigners can speak English. Sometimes I got the feeling that even if they did speak English they were not going to be accommodating, so I made sure I learned enough where I could get around.

A heartwarming experience was the time my husband and I took a trip to Italy to see if we could find some of my relatives on my father's side. I had more information about them and the location of where they lived. We stopped our car in the middle of town, and I got out and asked a group of men (all in dark suits), if they knew the name Sciarappa (my maiden name). They pointed to a home and told me to ask the lady there who might know. Three people appeared at the door. One was a young woman, another was a woman who appeared to be a grandmother, and there was a young child about nine years old. The young woman was attempting to explain to me the directions which she gathered I obviously did not understand. At that point she gestured, and I understood she was going to send the nine year old with us in our car to show us where to go. I could also see the grandmother quite upset with her daughter for letting her child go with strangers. I could make out and understand the young woman telling the grandmother not to worry because we had a USA sticker on the back of our window. All military people had to have this white and black sticker displayed in their car rear window. I was so proud of my country at that time that she felt confident enough to send her child with us just because we were from America.

We met the delightful relatives who indeed had a picture of my grandfather that I recognized. They invited us to stay overnight and to join their fest, but we were on a time schedule and could not. We did enjoy a drink and pastry with them however. The man in the family saw my English to Italian translation book and went and got his Italian to English book, and we had fun talking with each other. Another time, shortly after the 1986 bombing of Libya by the U.S., we drove to Rome from our home in Germany and then decided to rent a vehicle because we did not feel safe advertising with the USA sticker. Fortunately, this time, that was a good choice because the car was broken into. Since it was a rental vehicle, we were able to just switch cars at the rental agency and continue on our trip rather than having to wait around to have our own car fixed. Returning to our home in Dambach, Germany, we found security like never before, and we even had the military police guarding our home.

Upon reading the book *Frank Sinatra: History, Identity, and Italian American Culture* edited by Stanislao G. Pugliese, I noticed that Mr. Sinatra definitely experienced being called all those above mentioned negative names, but he fought back and he chose to represent the oppressed of many races long before it was fashionable to do so. He also refused to remove the vowel from his last name and kept it completely Italian. Because of Mr. Sinatra's tough guy image some Italian Americans did not idolize him though they appreciated his talent. Every weekend, and during different seasons, my aunts who were members of the "bobby sox" group (a name given to teenagers who wore saddle shoes and ankle socks) when Sinatra became famous, would group together and clean the house. That was one custom I did not want to inherit from them. I hated cleaning on my weekends off from work and eventually bought white furniture because then you could not see the dust as much. During the spring time (they called it spring cleaning) bright floral slip covers would be put over the darker colored couches, and the heavy drapes would come down from the windows and light airy curtains replaced them. The house would sparkle, and they had a lot of fun. They would crank the old Victrola (a record playing machine) and play Frank Sinatra tunes and also listen to the radio to station WNEW, and we would all sing together. Frank Sinatra was a big part of popular culture in my aunts' younger years, and they certainly enjoyed hearing the songs he sang. My aunts did not appear to be obsessed by Mr. Sinatra though as were many young girls during that time period. When the news media told about the young girls screaming and fainting when they saw Frank Sinatra, my aunts laughed and thought how foolish those other girls were, so I would not say that group of star struck girls was representative of all the girls of that time period. The stereotypical Italian American images do not always hold true in individual experiences. Many felt that Sinatra's slight build made the girls want to nurture him, and with so many men away fighting in the war Frank just seemed to be the perfect substitute man to idolize.

The two younger aunts, who were closer to my age, married at a young age. Aunt Margie (Margaret) was nineteen and my aunt Netta (Antoinette) was in her early twenties. They each had children, and I used to babysit for them. Each of them bought homes within walking distance of the house where they were raised and where we all lived together at one time. Aunt Rae (Rachel) was the oldest of the children in my grandmother's family and was married when I was born, so she did not live in the house with the rest of us at that time. However, her influence on me was very strong because she had no children of her own. She doted on me, the only grandchild. We would visit each other often wherever she happened to be living, and we communicated a lot by writing letters to one another. Aunt Jean (Jeannette) and I were very close. At one time we both worked at Fort Monmouth in New Jersey and would enjoy driving to work together talking about our jobs, popular culture, and the actions and excitement caused by the singing group the Beatles and the other famous singer of the day, Elvis Presley. All the sisters remained friends until the day they died.

Chapter Seventeen

Proud to be an Italian American

Including my Italian American heritage in my memoir was the idea of my Professor Cathy Stanton. I am so thrilled Cathy gave me this marvelous suggestion because I feel I learned a lot that I did not know. Part of this I am sure came from living in a small town and not a city. I also did not live among other Italians, so my expressions followed those of the friends with whom I associated. I have come to the conclusion that no matter the hardship or upbringing, Italian Americans have left their mark not only on their homeland of Italy and their new land of America, but in the world overall. Who does not know Sinatra, Springsteen, or Madonna? How about Michaelangelo or Leonardo DaVinci? How about the beautiful artwork of The Pieta and of the statue David? You may not know women like Sofonisba Anguissola, Lavinia Fontana, Artemisia Gentileschi, but let me assure you they are painters from the Renaissance to Baroque period whose works I have personally seen and can attest to their greatness. Their only disadvantage was they were never publicized as society was often wont to do where women were concerned, so I am doing it now. They are all Italian however, and were brave enough back in the 1500's to defy custom and become women painters. Their paintings often provided the money on which the family lived. In our country we have Geraldine Ferraro as the first woman Vice-Presidential candidate on a national party ticket, and Nancy Pelosi is the first woman Speaker of the House. Both women are Italian Americans. Some countries even co-opted our own Italians to make them their own, especially the French. You have only to read Nick J. Mileti's book *Closet Italians: A Dazzling Collection of Illustrious Italians with Non-Italian Names* to get the picture. The Emperor of France, Napoleon Bonaparte, was Italian. There is famed artist Georgia O'Keeffe. Georgia was named for Giorgio Totto, her maternal Italian grandfather. How about Sullivan from the famous duo Gilbert and Sullivan?

There is John Cabot, the famous navigator whose discoveries changed the map of the world. Also, Yves Montand, Edith Piaf, Susan Sarandon, Brooke Shields, Tony Bennett, Bernadette Peters, Ann Bancroft, Cindy Williams, Penny Marshall, Dana Reeve, Ashley Judd, Matt Le Blanc, Vin Diesel, Mary Lou Retton, Connie Stevens, Nicholas Cage and Hulk Hogan. (Mileti 2004). There are many, many more. I was astounded not only by their names, but by the genius of their inventions, their talents, and their outstanding creativity. Listed in the book were some of the greatest artists, doctors, and scholars of their time period and again in the world. Am I proud? You bet!

I was a different Italian because of where I lived. I spoke differently than other Italian Americans I met around the country. Phrases and innuendoes that were familiar to them were not familiar to me. When they would mention certain aspects of their lives, I realized those aspects were not recognizable to me. I actually just comprehended the reasons why this was so from writing my memoir and realizing that where I was raised was so totally different than a lot of Italians. Obviously the deep love and affection of my family members contributed to my positive attitude. Knowing I had relatives who played musical instruments, grandparents who listened to opera and exposed me to the arts, who were jolly and happy, also helped to give me my positive attitude and love of the arts. Is this something inherited in the genes, or shaped by one's upbringing? A lot of my disposition also must have been the fact that my life was not structured daily with rules and sports leagues where I might feel the need to rebel. Many afternoons we could just enjoy sitting on our front porches talking with friends and doing nothing. How many young people get the opportunity to do that today? As I said before, we did as we pleased as long as we did not get into trouble. I would have to guess that the reason I never look at things negatively and why I never suspect that things are bad for me is that I could see how my grandmother who lost five to seven children (I am not exactly sure) by death at ages like six months, thirteen years old and older, never appeared to be despondent or complained, nor did my mother who had the responsibility of raising me on her own, albeit with a loving family to support her. We learn by example. How could I react otherwise?

One's neighbors, community, the food one learns to eat, family customs, these all help to form one's particular ethnicity and identity. They all give us the total woman/man, and foster our rites of passage. It does not make one more Italian because they lived in Boston or Philadelphia or Hoboken. It does not make one less Italian because they are part black and part Italian like Kym Ragusa. We all have our place stamped on our heritage. My default would be that it is hard to sell a happy story to the publishing world. You would not find publishers knocking down my door to publish my memoir. Other Italian American authors I read asked us to reclaim our culture, but they don't understand. I am giving you my culture as I lived it. I need not reclaim my culture because I never gave it away.

What is our obsession with the macabre, tragedy or the dysfunctional family? We have psychologists like C. G. Jung, the founder of analytical thinking, examining humans and his beliefs in the collective unconscious. Perhaps we would all be better off if psychologists spent more time studying the happy person. Would it not be wonderful if we could bottle the ingredients my family used to help make me the happy person I am? Does this make me less Italian because of my non-traditional, non-stereotypical upbringing? I think not.

Sometimes life happens to people like me who did not set out seeking what to me has been a glamorous life. Having a pleasing status in society, without the hindrances and obligations of fame, were to me the perfect blend for a happy, delightful life, even if I did live my life in reverse.

Chapter Eighteen

Becoming an Author

I became aware of the biggest way I lived my life in reverse when I enrolled at Vermont College. In our two-week residency, I noticed there were many aspiring young authors who were doing it the right way and taking literature courses to expand their knowledge in the hopes of becoming an author. When I re-entered college I already had two books published, and a third was published during my first semester at Vermont. So, I became an author first, and then went to college to examine my skills as a writer. In all my desires throughout the years, I never considered becoming a writer. Frankly, I was so busy living I didn't really have the time to sit down and just write. Of course, today, the computer has greatly eased the task. I actually probably wrote more than most young people today because I came from the letter-writing generation. This was our most reliable way to communicate. As I explained in other parts of this story, I never hesitated to write to government officials or letters to the editor of newspapers if I thought there was an injustice done of some type, so in that sense I was a writer, and I was a journalist in high school working in conjunction with The Asbury Park Press newspaper.

One of our biggest fights as activists was while living in Maryland when they wanted to put a jail in our quiet little community near a Day Care Center and the Metro. The officials said by having the jail near the Metro it would be more convenient for family members of the convicts to come and visit them. No one seemed to care that if a prisoner escaped, the Metro could also be an easy getaway for the prisoner, or it would be very easy to take hostages at the Day Care Center. Now, we were not using the NIMBY (not in my back yard) mentality either. Our community hosted the school bus depot, the regional post office and many other facilities. I wrote to the paper explaining all this and requesting that the facility be put at the second choice out in the country, and to not dump everything in Derwood (our little town) saying "Don't

Dump in Derwood." Well, the newspapers picked up on the Don't Dump in Derwood slogan, making it the headline for the week. This slogan continues to pop up occasionally today.

My other passion is fighting for the military spouse. I realized as a young wife that should my husband die before me I would then receive the survivor benefit, but once I reached the age to collect social security the government would offset my social security money so that I would not get the total amount I earned. My social security check is money I earned on my own working record. My husband paid for the survivor benefit out of his own paycheck as a choice to cover me when he died. Once a military man dies, his paycheck stops. If the husband is not kind enough to take his own money to pay for this survivor benefit than the wife/husband of the military person would not be covered, and she would have no money. The two monetary situations had nothing to do with one another, and I felt it was most unfair for the government to take money away from one thing to compensate for the other. I wrote (along with many others) to government officials and military magazines, and the change could finally be coming shortly, but it has certainly taken a long time. Though I was never a big women's "libber," I have always been an advocate for women's rights in the work place and in equality in the pay check. I urge young women and spouses to get their own credit card in their own names and to establish their own credit. I am adamant about using the privilege of voting in all the elections. So many young women today don't realize that when I was young, people like my mother-in-law could not take out a loan at a bank, nor have a credit card of their own. Young women have to learn to be astute and knowledgeable, and I am forthcoming to them with my advice.

After I retired from working in the office of a gastroenterologist, I had a lot more time to walk. I love the outdoors and walking is my favorite form of exercise. I live in this wonderful little oasis of an area that is quite countrified while being surrounded by major highways that can take me to wonderful faraway places in minutes. When I walk I am among the birds, stray dogs, bunny rabbits and tons of deer. The smell of honeysuckle in the spring is delicious, and in some areas where I would walk I could smell the appetizing odors of ethnic meals being prepared by people of Indian, Irish, and Italian descent, and other ethnicities. This area in Maryland is a wonderful melting pot of people and religions. Each day I would see something and think I needed to write the children and tell them about what I had seen. I was used to sending them journals of trips we took because that way I could convey to the four of them and the grandchildren all at one time what had occurred without repeating it many times over the phone. My intention was to write another journal until I saw an article on entering a poem-writing contest of twenty lines only.

Poetry was the farthest thing from my mind, but then again I realized how perfect this would be for me to document my thoughts in a short, concise form and tell about my walk. The following is the poem I entered:

> My Walk
> The sights, the sounds, the smells
> "Step on a crack, break your mother's back"
> My Walk
> The new church steeple, fall foliage,
> Beautiful sunsets, deer in path, baby rabbits
> My Walk
> City sounds, sirens, dogs barking, traffic
> Country atmosphere, children laughing
> Opera Singer, families yelling
> My Walk
> Plenteous smells of curry, barbecue, Italian sauce
> Honeysuckle, cut grass, roses, fresh air
> My Walk
> Solitude time, comfort time, prayers to God
> Husband time, great conversation, argument time
> Money talk, friend time, topic news, children, spouses
> My Walk
> The sights, the sounds, the smells
> The stress relieving, exercise fulfilling,
> Best time of my day

Frankly, I prefer a poem that rhymes, so I don't know how I came up with this particular poem. Apparently, once you enter a contest your name gets forwarded to many places because the next thing I knew was that I was getting requests for more of my poetry to have put in anthologies. I started writing and have had many poems published both nationally and internationally. When I finally had about fifteen poems, I thought I was going great guns. I received a notice from a publisher saying that he had read some of my poems, and would I like to have them published into a book at no cost to me. I was just too thrilled because I know books of poetry are not popular for being published as opposed to a novel. I immediately called the number, and we were discussing all the details. The lady asked me how many poems I had. When I told her only fifteen she did not laugh, but she said I would need at least sixty, or at least enough poems to fill sixty pages of a book. I told her I might be dead by the time I had sixty pages, so she suggested I print a book myself by going to a Kinko's or some such store. I had a store nearby at that time that was called Budget Printers, and they enjoyed helping me. This first book, because of its tiny size, I just published for family as Christmas gifts and they were a big hit (or so they said). Then I started to get serious about really publishing a book and looked into the various aspects of either hiring an agent, or using a company that helps to self-publish. The second choice gave you more control over your book, but they were also more careless about proof reading. I am really proud of the second book called *Grandmother's Jewels II*, but there were mistakes made in the printing that made me feel terrible until I read a book by Donald Trump where I spotted an error or two. Then, I figured, with all his money he could afford the best publishers in the country, and they still made mistakes, so I didn't feel quite so badly anymore.

A publisher that has had many number one books on the market published my third book. I wrote this book with a pen name for personal reasons–a very nice Italian pen name. The only disappointment I had with this publisher is they only make their books one size and if they had made my book smaller, the book itself would not have been so thin in content. This is a book about eighteen year olds and the fact they are considered adults at that age, another subject that is a passion of mine. Parents are paying the college tuitions, but unless the eighteen year old signs a form giving the parents' permission, if the student gets bad grades the parent will not be notified. This is a great injustice where I am concerned, among other things on that subject. Oddly, as I write this in April of 2007, the massacre has occurred at Virginia Tech University. The very issue I was complaining about above, student privacy, has now become more publicized since apparently the killer had issues that because of student privacy (even though the killer was older) could not be revealed. Now, I am even more outraged.

Someone wanting to know if I had any poems that could be made into songs also approached me. I received a letter in the mail with this request. My first intention was to throw it into the wastebasket when I heard someone on the radio singing the words, "Round, Round, I get around," by the Beach Boys. I could not help but think that I could certainly write something similar, so I sent a letter to the company asking for more information. They sent me a contract that was going to involve me paying some money up front. I read the contract carefully and contacted the Better Business Bureau. They basically only had some minor complaints, so I thought it might be worth taking a chance after having my husband review the contract as well. The cost did not warrant my seeing a lawyer, and we were not so dumb we did not know what to examine. I arranged to pay them in partial payments. That way, if I didn't like the work as we were progressing along the way, I would not be out of all my money. They were located in California near Hollywood, so it was necessary for me to be vigilant since we were coasts apart.

The money I paid turned out to be money well spent and rather small in retrospect, considering the finished product. Where else was I going to get a singer and full orchestra (band) arrangement for someone like myself and have the work put on a CD for publication and sale? Sometimes I didn't like their choice of singer for my song, or perhaps they might change the melody a little, but they were taking a risk as well, and there was no way I was ever going to get anyone else interested. You will notice that most famous singers publish their own words and songs, and perhaps you might only like one song on the entire CD. They published five songs for me. I always enjoy having my own tax ID number and getting my very small royalty checks. The last song they did was around "9/11" and they had some production problems because of the effects of a scarcity of a product that was a direct cause of the terrorism in New York City. This delayed production, and by that time I was on to other things. The last song was one of my favorites though when it finally came out and the perfect song to be played at my fiftieth wedding anniversary party called *"How Can I Go On."*

I learned a lot about the publishing business and what they are looking for in a book. I know the value of a copyright. I also know that most of us are not going to be wealthy from our writings like Joanne Kathleen Rowling, so we should learn to be realistic. Actually, as a woman, I am disappointed that author J. K. Rowling chose to use her initials instead of her name. I can only speculate why she did use her initials instead of her name. Was it perhaps because she felt by using her initials the readers would not know if she were a man or woman? Since her storyline portrayed wizardry she might have felt the public would find a male author more believable. Considering the effort involved for women authors to get their works published, one would think Joanne Kathleen would have been proud to come forth as a woman author. You can see I am a strong advocate for women's rights.

The work of many poets is quite intense. In my opinion, writing their poetry helps them to get rid of the hurt and anxiety they encounter in their lives. I perceive it to be of psychological help to them, when they document their feelings. When I write something intense it is more because of a world situation like "9/11" than a personal situation. Since I see no value on focusing on the negative things in my life, most of my poems fit the pattern of "happy poet." The following is a paragraph I wrote to conclude a story I composed for a college course, but it really helps to explain my venture into writing–even if I did do it without training and in reverse of the "norm."

> *I am fortunate to live in a country where freedom of speech and performance are encouraged and not banned. We can use the written word to express our points of view, to reprimand a wrong, and to praise things we think are worthy of praise. The various and many jobs I held, during my life, gave me ample opportunity to use what meager writing skills I have to get the job done. These skills could be used in writing a report, preparing a thesis, or typing an engi-*

neering specification. The same skills also were used in composing correspondence, writing a poem, or writing a short story for entertainment purposes. In learning about the famous women authors who came before me, I became enlightened and appreciative that they forged a way for me and all other women. They made it easier for women today to achieve. I appreciate the art of being able to learn to speak our language fluently and of having the knowledge to effectively document my thoughts by writing.

My grandparents read the Italian newspapers frequently and learned to speak and write English. To me, anyone who can speak more than one language is brilliant, and that is how I feel about my grandparents. They became United States citizens, and I can remember my grandmother studying to take her test. When we took her to Mexico one year after she became a citizen of the United States, we had to declare our country of citizenship. She sure was proud when she looked out the window of the car and said to the man "A you, a sssss, a aay." USA indeed! This is why it gives me such a thrill to now be able to write about my own life and show the part my family members had in making me who I am today.

Chapter Nineteen

Some Fascinating Women

I must not finish my story without giving due credit to those two women aunts in my life, besides my mother and grandmother, whose influence had a great affect on me. They taught me good manners, corrected my grammar and gave me my positive attitude along with lots of love. They were not complainers, and they had self-confidence. You cannot help to have all these good qualities rub off on you when you live in close proximity to one another, or keep in close contact. I learned the proper way to eat soup by saying, "Like a ship goes out to sea, I push my spoon away from me." Who would have thought? These two older aunts (Rae and Jean) were the ones that exuded the greatest influence. They were immaculate in appearance and known throughout the town for their fashion expertise and style. They would make fresh lemonade in the summer and fresh orange juice too using a cone shaped bowl that had a rim to catch the juice after squeezing the fruit. When I was little and it got really hot out, the aunts filled a big metal tub with water which was my version of today's plastic swimming pool. The elder Aunt Rae smelled like lavender and Jean, the younger one, had the delightful odor of talcum powder that many women used in those days. One brand I remember was Cashmere Bouquet. This was even though they both had bottles of Chanel Number Five perfume sitting on their dressers. One was married to a handsome man that everyone loved. He was the one from Alfred, New York.

The other aunt remained single though she was lovely and had the most gorgeous figure ever. She would go dancing at the block parties, and too many married men would say to her, "Oh, man, if I only did not have a wife," as they asked her to dance. She had many fitting suitors, but I suspect from some overheard conversations that she fell in love with a married man and would not let him date her or have an affair as she respected the institution of marriage. When she reached a certain age I remember her just deciding that she had lived a good life, had by then plenty of nieces and nephews to spoil and enjoy like her own children, and she did not need a man to fulfill her. She drove around in her fancy Cadillac and wore her ocelot coat (when it was quite all right to wear fur). She collected Iladro figurines, some as big as three to four feet tall. When it came time to settle her estate they mysteriously disappeared. She was the executive administrative officer for over seven Generals of the Army at Fort Monmouth in New Jersey.

Sadly, she and my grandmother (who I already said lived to be 102 years old) were stricken with Alzheimer's in their later years. This is such a heartbreaking disease, and I had several uncles who also suffered from it. I might suspect that some of my urge to study is to keep my mind active in the hopes of fending off this horrible disease. One evening, my aunt kept taking out this ball gown to show me. People with Alzheimer's often repeat things or do things repetitively. She reminded me that she wore it to a ball in Venezuela where she dated a military officer while visiting her sister and brother-in-law. I would tell her it was lovely, and then she would bring it out again, and again I would tell her it was lovely. Around the fifth time I just said, "Oh, your friend really liked the dress." She pops back, "No, he liked what was in the dress." There are times I guess when those Alzheimer's minds just get right to the point. My young cousin and his wife were in their forties, and had three small children of their own, but they cared for the then-widowed aunt, the single aunt, and my grandmother until the day they died at the home where I was raised. Other cousins of mine also helped. Unfortunately, I did not live nearby, but did what I could. My cousins cleaned their home and saw that they were fed, and they were never put in a nursing home.

During Thanksgiving and other big eating holidays all the women would help in the kitchen while the men picked the quills out of the turkey. My aunts loved to have the fanciest of table decorations with all the best silver and china, and this tradition I carry on today. I really do not know why we were not all huge in size. The meal was out of this world. We would start off with an appetizer, like a cup of fresh cut up fruit, and sometimes soup. Then we would be served an antipasto. After that came the pasta with sausages, meatballs and some wonderful rolled meat called brociole that was tied and cooked in a sauce, and a salad. Just when you thought you were going to burst, out would come the turkey, creamed peas and carrots, mashed potatoes, sweet potatoes and corn, and I am sure I am leaving something out. Then of course came all the pastries, pies and bowls of fresh fruit. Grace was always said before meals, and we sure had a lot for which to be thankful.

I felt the best way I could honor these women was to give them this tribute in my first book *Grandmother's Jewels* by saying,

This book is lovingly dedicated to five beautiful women

Ruth Helena Sciarappa–Who gave me life, love and taught me the meaning of hard work–You were taken from me much too young.

Philomena Mazzei–A wonderful grandmother who gave me a zest for life and taught me to respect all members of society.

Rachel Witter–A special aunt who taught me assertiveness and proper etiquette.

Jeannette Mazzei–Another special aunt who taught me compassion and gentility.

Catherine Griswold–A super mother-in-law who taught me how to do it all with class.

And last but not least to my wonderful husband

William Griswold–Who has been there through the good times and the bad, my rock, my lover and my best friend.

Epilogue

On July 18, 2007, at seven o'clock in the evening, Lucille received her Bachelor of Arts Degree from the Vermont College of Union Institute and University at Montpelier, Vermont. It was the night before her fifty-forth wedding anniversary. The graduates were led into College Hall by a bagpiper. As adult graduates, each student could choose to wear whatever color cap and gown they desired, and Lucille and her friend Jheremy from Maryland chose white. They were the oldest and the youngest graduates, and they both lived near each other in Maryland. Jheremy and Lucille met only after they enrolled at the Vermont College online program. Jheremy's parents were late coming to the graduation because they got lost. So, Jheremy's children merely sat on their mother's lap upon the stage with the rest of the graduates. When the parents finally arrived, the proceedings simply stopped until the transfer of children from the mother to the grandparents was completed. Not one person complained. Jheremy's children handed their mother her degree and Lucille, of course, chose her husband Bill to do the honors. Each graduate had the opportunity to get behind the microphone to say anything they pleased. The singer, with her pink ukulele, had all the graduates doing their own little dance on stage. Outside of attending all her family's wonderful graduations, Lucille felt that the July 18, 2007, graduation was the best graduation ever.

Lucille and Bill celebrated their fifty-fifth wedding anniversary parasailing over the shores of Ocean City, Maryland.

Bibliography

DeSalvo, Louise. *Crazy in the Kitchen: Foods, Feuds and Forgiveness in an Italian American Family.* New York: Bloomsbury, Publishing, 2004.

Ets, Maria Hall. *Rosa: The Life of an Italian Immigrant.* Madison, Wisconsin: University of Wisconsin Press, 1970.

Ferraro, Thomas J. *Feeling Italian: The Art of Ethnicity in America.* New York: NYU Press, 2005.

Fiorina, Carly. *Tough Choices: A Memoir.* New York: Penquin Group, 2006.

Gans, Herbert. *The Urban Villagers: Group and Class in the Life of Italian Americans.* New York: Free Press, 1982.

Guinta, Edvige. *Writing with an Accent: Contemporary Italian American Women Authors.* New York: Palgrave, 2002.

Heilbrun, Carolyn G. *Writing a Woman's Life.* New York: W. W. Norton & Company, 1988.

Holmes, Frank R. (ED.). *The History of Monmouth County, New Jersey 1664-1920.* New York: Lewis Historical Publishing Company, 1922.

Luconi, Stefano. *From Paesani to White Ethnics: The Italian Experience in Philadelphia.* Albany, New York: State University of New York Press, 2001.

Mileti, Nick J. *Closet Italians: A Dazzling Collection of Illustrious Italians with Non Italian Names.* Philadelphia, PA: Xlibris Corporation, 2004.

Pugliese, Stanislao G. (Ed.). *Frank Sinatra History, Identity, and Italian American Culture.* New York: Palgrave MacMillan, 2004.

Ragusa, Kym. *The Skin Between Us: A Memoir of Race, Beauty, and Belonging.* New York: W. W. W. Norton & Company, 2006.

www.ingramcontent.com/pod-product-compliance
Lightning Source LLC
Chambersburg PA
CBHW031554300426
44111CB00006BA/313